GLOBAL BARGAIN HUNTING

The Investor's Guide to Profits in Emerging Markets

Burton G. Malkiel

and

J. P. Mei

SIMON & SCHUSTER

SIMON & SCHUSTER
Rockefeller Center
1230 Avenue of the Americas
New York, NY 10020

SIMON & SCHUSTER and colophon are registered trademarks
of Simon & Schuster Inc.

Designed by Irving Perkins Associates

Manufactured in the United States of America

1   3   5   7   9   10   8   6   4   2

Library of Congress Cataloging-in-Publication Data

Malkiel, Burton G.
Global bargain hunting : the investor's guide to profits in
emerging markets / Burton G. Malkiel and J. P. Mei.
p.   cm.
Includes index.
1. Investments, Foreign—Developing countries.
2. Securities—Developing countries.   I. Mei, J. P.   II. Title.
HG5993.M348   1998
332.67'3'091724—dc21   97-29744
                                                         CIP
ISBN 0-684-83518-5

The authors gratefully acknowledge the following for permission to reprint this
material: Agence France-Presse for the photograph of the Petronas Towers and
"High Fashion in China"; Bruce Beattie and the Copley News Service for the
"We're Out of Power" cartoon; Ken Alexander and the *San Francisco Examiner*
for the "Bankruptcy" cartoon; Morris E. Docktor for the "Taiwan Stock Market"
cartoon; A/P Wide World Photos for the photograph of Mori Shanghai Tower;
Morningstar for the "T. Rowe Price Fund" detail page from *Ascent*.

For Nancy and Jonathan,
Wei and Grayce

Contents

PART III: HOW TO INVEST IN EMERGING MARKETS

CHAPTER SEVEN:
The Professionally Managed Approach
129

CHAPTER EIGHT:
The Indexed, or Computer-Managed, Approach
149

CHAPTER NINE:
The Self-Directed Approach: Actively Managing
Your Emerging-Market Portfolio
165

CHAPTER TEN:

Bargains in Bonds, Real Estate, and Natural Resources
185

CHAPTER ELEVEN:

Investment Strategies and Specific Recommendations
208

GLOBAL
BARGAIN
HUNTING

Preface

As the sun begins to rise on foggy mornings in Dhaka, Bangladesh, thousands of women in colorful saris walk along the causeway from the Baridara section of the city to a group of buildings that make up the city's garment district. The women sit at sewing machines all day, making a variety of textile products that range from track suits to windbreakers. These products reach an estimated one in every five American homes, and their wholesale value in the late 1990s was more than $1.5 billion. Neither the factories nor their products existed when these women were born.

Bangladesh, with its 120 million people, has long been ranked as one of the poorest countries in the world. Once described by Henry Kissinger as an "international basket case," Bangladesh changed in the 1990s. After years of coups and military rule, an elected civilian government led a transition to a free-market economy. Since then, progress has been nothing short of remarkable. From 1989 to 1996, per capita income doubled, and increased numbers of families now earn sufficient income from their work to be able to pay for food, rent, and clothing. The economic gains from growth have been distributed not only to businesses, whose profits have soared, but also to labor, whose real take-home income has been increasing at several times the growth rates in western Europe and the United States.

With increased prosperity have come actions by business, labor unions, and the Bangladeshi government to curb the use of child labor in the garment factories and to provide improved schooling opportunities for children. While the poverty of the country is still desperate by Western standards, living conditions have improved more during the 1990s than in the forty years before.

Today, we call Bangladesh an "emerging market," Wall Street's politically correct name for what used to be called a "less developed country." Its economic story is not an isolated one. From Chile to China, formerly less developed countries are experiencing an economic expansion that is several times greater than the growth rates in the West. Their markets offer today's most exciting investment opportunities and form the third millennium's investment frontier.

The Bangladeshis' dream of prosperity and continued growth, however, is a fragile one. The country's leading politicians have been unable to rise above the civil war enmities that dismembered it from Pakistan in 1971. It is walking a tightrope characterized by political turmoil, violence, widespread strikes, and the ever-present fear of a new army coup. Ethnic Bengalis' age-old factions are as much a part of their inheritance as is their penchant for philosophy and poetry. A newspaper editor described the situation in 1996 as one of being "in the grip of a government without credibility, and an opposition without responsibility." Whether the democratic parliamentary government, which has provided the essential spur to economic growth, will survive is far from certain.

The case of Bangladesh is an excellent illustration of both the attractive possibilities that are associated with investments in emerging markets and the enormous risks involved. The purpose of this book is to describe both the rewards and the risks of these investments as fully and clearly as possible and to explain a strategy that will minimize those risks. It will take us on a grand adventure along the newest investment frontier, an adventure that no serious investor will want to miss or can afford to ignore.

A Road Map of the Hunt

We believe that the securities of companies in emerging markets represent extraordinary opportunities for profitable investment. Part I lays out our arguments. We will show why we believe these securities offer investors a chance to get in on the ground floor of the most exciting growth opportunities in the world at bargain-basement prices.

The opportunity for large gains from investments in emerging markets does come with a price: extreme risk. The stock markets of developing countries are extraordinarily volatile and buffeted by a variety of special risks, from political instability to currency upheavals. When sending investment funds abroad into some emerging markets, there is a risk that the trip will be one-way. In Part II, we explain the characteristics of these risks to forewarn investors of the dangerous terrain. Most important, we present a strategy whereby investors can contain the risks of emerging-market investing while simultaneously increasing their returns.

Part III is a how-to manual. Here we present a step-by-step guide to enable any individual to access the exciting opportunities we foresee from the purchase of emerging-market securities. Anyone with an interest in investing can easily follow our advice. So join us on a global bargain-hunting adventure where we will find the most exciting investment opportunities in the world!

PART I

THE RICHES
TO BE REAPED

As we are so insistent that global bargain hunters include emerging markets in their investment safaris, it is only right that we first state what we mean by the term. It was coined by the World Bank's International Finance Corporation (IFC) to describe any country whose per capita income was less than $8,956 in 1994. (Countries with higher per capita incomes, by the way, are said to be "developed" rather than "emerged.") The U.S. investment firm Morgan Stanley liked the term but disagreed with the definition. In Morgan Stanley's lexicon, an emerging country is one in which growth and "a process of change" are under way; thus, a poor country that is stagnant does not qualify as an emerging market.

Our own classification of "emerging markets" is slightly broader than that of the IFC because we have also included Hong Kong and Singapore. There are two main reasons. First, these two economies are deeply rooted in the emerging economies of Asia, with many of their listed companies generating a significant amount of their earnings from neighboring emerging markets. Second, both of these equity markets are growing as rapidly as other emerging markets, and they offer world investors an alternative way of benefiting from the growing economies of China, Indonesia, Malaysia, Thailand, and other Asian countries. As a result, most managers of emerging-market investment funds include Hong Kong and Singapore stocks in their portfolios.

No matter what definition one uses, however, there is a brilliance about the growth statistics of these markets. Annual economic output in Asia grew at close to 10 percent during the 1990s and is forecast by the World Bank to continue to grow into the twenty-first century at 7.5 percent. While the second figure might at first glance appear to represent a slowdown, it is actually three times the forecast for the economies of the developed world. Growth in Latin America and eastern Europe, while far slower than in Asia, is forecast to be almost twice as fast as in the West. Similarly, corporate profits are expected to increase far more swiftly in emerging markets than in mature Western economies.

We base our enthusiasm on more than forecasts, however, as economic analysis strongly buttresses our point. Of course, there are many who feel that economics makes no contribution to investment decision making. The legendary investment manager Peter Lynch is in this camp and is said to have quipped that if investors spent fourteen minutes a year on economic analysis, they would have wasted twelve of them. The Nobel Prize Committee disagreed. In 1990, it presented the award in economics to Harry Markowitz for his development of "portfolio theory." This is the theory that underlies our belief that every investment portfolio should include some exposure to emerging-market securities.

We will also make our case with a few critical facts and figures. While George Bernard Shaw suggested that the mark of a truly educated person is a deep interest in statistics, we will hold the numerical analysis defending our recommendations to the barest minimum. Anyone with an interest in improved portfolio performance will easily be able to follow our argument. In the process, we hope to show that the term "lucid economist" is not an oxymoron.

The chapters in Part I review the financial attractions within emerging markets. We show first that these budding markets provide far greater growth opportunities for investors than the gray-haired developed economies are likely to muster. Next, we indicate that this greater growth is often available at far more attractive prices than those in the sky-high U.S. stock market or those of other developed markets. Then, we suggest (and more fully develop in Part II) that even though the common stocks from emerging market countries are themselves much riskier than the equities from developed markets, the inclusion of emerging market assets can paradoxically result in *lower* portfolio risk. While today one finds few schools of U.S. and western European investors swimming overseas, we will show why it is likely that this will change. We believe increasing flows of funds will soon spread into emerging markets and thus create extremely favorable conditions for potentially large capital gains.

CHAPTER ONE

Investment Opportunities Flourish Outside the Developed World

GROWTH IN SALES and earnings is the most important element in determining the financial rewards from investing in common stocks. As the owner of a company's stock, you are also part owner of the business and share in the success of the enterprise in terms of any dividends the company distributes. It also means that if the company does well and the price of the shares appreciates, you earn a capital gain. When professionals talk about the total return from stock ownership, they combine the returns that come from dividends and the capital gains that result from any increase in the price of the shares.

The simple truth is that by far the greatest total returns from stock ownership today are located in the emerging markets of the world. While there will continue to be financially rewarding opportunities for investments in more mature markets—particularly in companies that exploit opportunities in developing countries—the greatest growth will come from firms actually based in the emerging markets.

This trend represents a flip-flop. In the nineteenth century, Great Britain and Europe dominated the world in economics, culture, and power. The twentieth century was the "age of America," a century in which the United States became the world's great superpower. In the twenty-first century, however, this Western monopoly will be shattered by the rise of the world's emerging markets. Growth in these markets promises to far surpass the economic miracle spawned by the Industrial Revolution at the end of the nineteenth century.

The size of these markets alone is staggering. Based on the IFC definition, they contain 85 percent of the world's population. Their combined gross domestic product (GDP) is currently only about 21 percent of the world's total production of goods and services, but that share is likely to increase substantially. In addition, their equity markets are just beginning to take shape, accounting in 1996 for only 11 percent of the world's total market value of equities (including Hong Kong and Singapore, which we do in our definition of emerging markets, would boost this figure to 14 percent). Figure 1-1 displays the relative sizes of developed and emerging markets.

In Asia alone, wealth is being generated on a scale and with a speed that is probably without historical precedent. The number of non-Japanese multimillionaires is expected to exceed 1 million before the turn of the century. Billionaires are springing up from Taiwan to Thailand, from India to Indonesia, and from Hong Kong to Kuala Lumpur. To find even a close precedent for so remarkable a leap from rags to riches, one needs to revisit the history of the United States at the end of the nineteenth century. But Asia is getting richer more quickly than any other region at any time in history.

Good News from Recent Investors

Unadorned statistics describing the rapid increases in output of emerging-market economies are staggering. Figure 1-2 presents ten-year growth rates for a variety of Asian and Latin American economies compared with that of the United States, which is representative of the developed world. The economies of East Asia have been growing at more than three times the rate of growth in the United States. If growth continues into the twenty-first century

FIGURE 1-1

Emerging Markets' Share of World Population, Gross Domestic Products,* and Market Value of Common Stocks, 1996

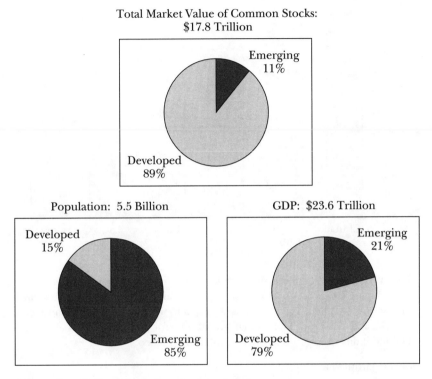

Total Market Value of Common Stocks:
$17.8 Trillion

Emerging
11%

Developed
89%

Population: 5.5 Billion

Developed
15%

Emerging
85%

GDP: $23.6 Trillion

Emerging
21%

Developed
79%

* The value of all goods and services produced.

at anything near its recent rate (as we will argue is likely), six of the top ten economies of the world will be in Asia. This group encompasses China, Japan, India, Indonesia, South Korea, and Thailand. Only two European countries, Germany and France, will make the list. In addition, rapid rates of growth have begun in the formerly Communist countries of eastern Europe, such as Poland, Hungary, and the Czech Republic. Even Latin America, stagnant for much of the 1970s and '80s and suffering severe economic setbacks in the early 1990s, has been growing at significantly more rapid rates than its northern neighbor.

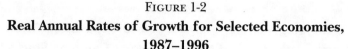

FIGURE 1-2

Real Annual Rates of Growth for Selected Economies, 1987–1996

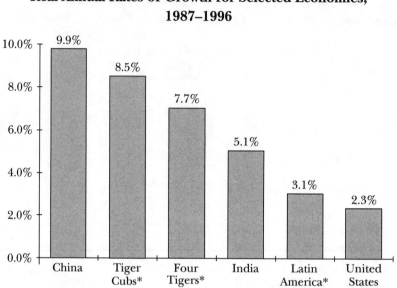

*The average growth rate for the so-called Four Tigers is an equally weighted index of Hong Kong, South Korea, Singapore, and Taiwan. The average growth rate for the so-called Tiger Cubs is an equally weighted index of Indonesia, Malaysia, and Thailand. The average growth rate for Latin America is an equally weighted index of Argentina, Brazil, Chile, and Mexico.

SOURCE: Jardine Fleming.

Rapid economic growth creates an environment where business firms can themselves grow and prosper. While this seems blatantly obvious, the investment firm of Smith Barney used data from the 1970s to the 1990s to measure the relationship between a country's growth and its broad stock market index. Smith Barney confirmed that the more rapid the economic growth, the greater the market returns. The relationship between export growth and stock returns is especially strong. Since stockholder returns come from both dividends and gains in the price of the shares, it is natural to expect such a relationship to continue as long as the initial valuation levels of the shares are reasonable. As can be seen in Figure 1-3, the rapid growth in economic output has, in fact, been associated with extraordinary investment returns in the stock markets of many emerging economies. Even during a decade when the U.S. market experienced returns almost 50 percent greater than its long-run 10 percent average, several emerging markets easily outdistanced U.S. stock returns. Moreover, the valuation levels for many of the emerging stock markets remain relatively low, suggesting that attractive future returns are a reasonable expectation. For this reason, our unequivocal advice to investors is to go where the growth is: in building a portfolio, do not ignore emerging markets.

FIGURE 1-3

Average Annual Dollar Returns for the Ten Years Ended December 31, 1996*

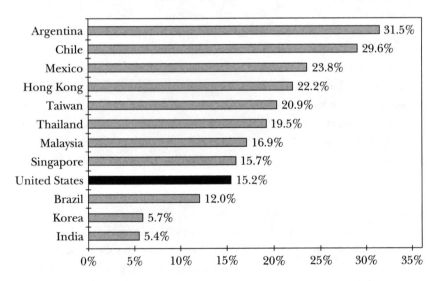

During one of the best decades in history for common stock returns in the United States, several emerging stock markets have provided substantially larger total returns.

*Returns include capital gains and dividends.

SOURCE: International Finance Corporation.

Emerging Markets Around the World

Let us now take a closer look at the emerging-market landscape and zoom in on specific regions and countries. These are grouped and presented by their relative economic strength as we write today.

Four Tigers: Hong Kong, South Korea, Singapore, and Taiwan

By any measure, the unexpected success of the "Four Tigers" is extraordinary. In 1960, when economists at the World Bank offered their predictions about the economic future of various Asian economies, none of the four was considered promising. In many ways, their economic takeoff reads like a Cinderella story:

Once upon a time there was a small British colony named Hong Kong. Mother Nature did not like Hong Kong. She made it a small rocky place with few resources and let it be flooded with millions of refugees. Its climate was hot and rainy, and it was often devastated by severe storms—tropical as well as political. Although most people had neither jobs nor shelter, and often even no food, they worked very hard and dreamed of a better life.

Hong Kong had two Asian neighbors. Their names were India and the Philippines, and they were full of promise. Mother Nature loved these two countries and gave them many natural and human resources. Both countries had democratic politicians, eloquent lawyers, well-trained civil servants, and lots of economists. India seemed to have everything going for it. The Philippines was the richest country in Southeast Asia—so rich that in the mid-1950s, thousands of Hong Kong women flocked to Manila to work as maids. To the World Bank, it appeared that these two countries were destined for prosperity, while Hong Kong's dream would never come true.

Then the Grand Duke of Capitalism called, and India, the Philippines, and Hong Kong were asked to try on the glass slipper called "free-market development." The thick socks of socialism made it impossible for India to put her feet into the slipper, and the Philippines was not interested because Mrs. Marcos already had too many pairs of shoes. Hong Kong thought it was too poor to even try, but the Grand Duke persuaded her to put her foot into the glass slipper, and it fit perfectly. So Hong Kong went to the Castle of Capitalism, and she lived there happily ever after.

Since then, the fortunes of Hong Kong and its two neighbors have reversed. Forty years later, Hong Kong became one of the richest places in the world with an output of goods and services of $22,000 per capita, many times higher than the $1,280 of India and the $2,600 of the Philippines. With one-tenth the population of the Philippines, Hong Kong exported eight times more goods in 1996 than the Philippines and five times more than India. As a result of this change in economic status, more than 100,000 Filipino maids worked in Hong Kong during the later 1990s. Some were even hired by those Hong Kong women who used to work in Manila.

This may sound like a fairy tale, but it is the true story of the rise of modern Hong Kong. And roughly the same rags-to-riches Cinderella story occurred in South Korea, Singapore, and Taiwan as well.

South Korea is perhaps an even better story. In the aftermath of the devastation of the Korean War, South Korea was dirt poor and on the verge of starvation. Its income in 1960 was less than $100 per person. North Korea, on the other hand, was in much better shape. When the truce agreement was signed, the 38th Parallel left most of the region's industrial facilities in the North. With richer mineral resources and a much better infrastructure, it seemed that the North was destined to do much better economically than the South. Some forty years later, however, the fortunes of the two countries could not have been more different. After decades of free-market development, South Korea has become a world manufacturing powerhouse. After decades of Communist mismanagement, North Korea was on the verge of economic collapse during the last half of the 1990s. Today, South Korea, while hardly free of problems, is the tenth largest exporting nation in the world with a per capita output of over $10,000.

The other two tigers, Singapore and Taiwan, had similar humble beginnings. Rejected by the Malaysian Federation in 1965, the newly independent city-state of Singapore was like a penniless orphan left outside in the cold. Most experts doubted that the small state, with no natural resources and little industrial base, could survive. But private enterprise was allowed to flourish under the strong leadership of Prime Minister Lee Kuan Yew. Thirty years after independence, Singapore has become the most prosperous city in the world.

The economic race between Taiwan and China was probably the most unequal match in world history. In 1950, Taiwan was a small island flooded with millions of refugees and defeated Nationalist troops. China, on the other hand, was 250 times larger in land mass and had fifty times the population of Taiwan. Thirty years later, however, the tiny capitalist Taiwan had far outdistanced the giant Communist mainland. In 1980, at the beginning of Deng Xiaoping's plan to transform the Chinese economy, little Taiwan had more foreign exchange reserves than China, and its per capita income was more than ten times greater.

These real-life Cinderella success stories have one important difference from the fairy tale. Cinderella was given a happy and bountiful life ever after in the castle because she married the Prince. The Four Tigers achieved their good lives the old-fashioned way— they earned it. As a matter of fact, their welfare and social security programs were far from generous, and the population of these countries *had* to work hard and save for a rainy day on their own. It is no wonder that all four Tigers have savings rates double or triple those in the United States. These high savings rates made it possible for businesses in these countries to raise the capital needed for domestic growth rather than relying on foreign sources. Indeed, these four small economies together exported almost the same total value of goods in 1996 as the United States did. Their economic success enriched not only their own people but world investors as well.

To be sure, in many cases the governments of these countries have intervened selectively in the development process. But as the World Bank has pointed out, while there have been differences in the intervention process, the common theme of the Asian experience is that governments have used a "market-friendly" approach to economic development. Government activism has been limited and has relied primarily on free-market development. As William McDonough, president of the Federal Reserve Bank of New York, explained, "such interventions have been aimed generally at addressing market inadequacies or outright failures in resource allocation. More importantly, the industries have been put to the discipline of domestic and international market competition. And, usually, when the costs of interventions have become excessive—as, for example, in the case of a heavy chemicals industry drive in South Korea—governments have pulled back." As a consequence, unleashing the incentives of the free market has been the overarching theme of the Tigers' development.

The success of the Four Tigers has demonstrated to all developing countries that if they put on the glass slipper of free-market development—together with hard work, high savings, and prudent entitlement programs—their dreams of modernization can also come true.

Three Tiger Cubs: Malaysia, Indonesia, and Thailand

Roughly ten years after the economic takeoff of the Four Tigers, three more Asian countries chose the glass slipper of free-market development and started their journey toward modernization. While their governments often pursued different development policies, Malaysia, Indonesia, and Thailand have all relied primarily on free-market incentives and, in the last twenty years, have produced economic miracles.

Malaysia and Thailand were the first to achieve the growth standards set by the Four Tigers. Malaysia is a diverse country with several large ethnic groups, roughly 60 percent Malay, 32 percent Chinese, and 8 percent East Indian, with small numbers of Indonesians, Thais, and Europeans. Despite occasional ethnic tension, Malaysia has demonstrated to the world how people of different ethnic groups can cooperate to achieve prosperity in a free-market system. Symbolic of Malaysia's reach for the stars, the world's tallest building (pictured below) rises in the modern city of Kuala Lumpur.

Petronas Towers, Kuala Lumpur

The World's Tallest Building and a Monument Symbolic of Malaysia's Development

Thailand began as an agricultural society well known for its rice, rubber, and buffalos wandering in fields. Since 1975, however, rapid economic development—spawned by a culture of free enterprise—has changed the country into a prime manufacturing center of the Far East. Prosperity has produced tens of thousands of millionaires and congested city streets full of Mercedeses and BMWs. Today, Thailand is well known among world travelers for its Comfort 100s—portable car toilets indispensable for sitting through Bangkok's traffic jams.

Indonesia is the youngest of the three Tiger Cubs since its full-scale economic reform did not start until the mid-1980s. It is the fourth most populous nation in the world after China, India, and the United States. In the 1950s, it was one of the poorest countries on earth. As President Richard Nixon observed of his trip there as vice president, ". . . as we drove through the streets of Jakarta, then the world's most densely populated city, we saw open sewers emptying into canals. Children were swimming in the filthy water. Women were doing their laundry in it." While there is still much poverty, a great deal of progress has been made since then. Today's Jakarta is like any other major Asian commercial center, bustling with commercial activity and with glass skyscrapers dominating the skyline.

The Tiger Cubs, however, are not without growth pains. In 1997, an overvalued currency and large trade deficit triggered a currency crisis in Thailand, which quickly spilled over to Malaysia and Indonesia. While the cubs stand a good chance to recover, investors will be watching in agony as they go through the teething process.

One Dragon: China

At the end of 1978, the roars of the tigers and tiger cubs finally woke a sleeping dragon: China. After decades of political persecution and economic stagnation under Chairman Mao Zedong, it was nothing short of a revolution when Chinese leader Deng Xiaoping proclaimed a new Communist manifesto to the world: To get rich is glorious.

Free-market reform has completely changed China since 1978. During the next eighteen years, it recorded an amazing 10 percent growth in output per year. Although the Four Tigers had a similar growth rate during their economic takeoff, as Nicholas Kristof observed, "together they are no more than the size of a Chinese province." As a result of this economic growth, a rural population of 170 million has been lifted out of poverty. More than 120 million new jobs—equivalent to the entire U.S. workforce—have been created, and most of these jobs are in the private sector of the economy. And the free-market reform has changed millions of people who were paupers under the old Communist system into prosperous entrepreneurs. The open-door policy has also integrated ancient China into the modern world. It has brought in Big Macs, CNN, the Internet, Michael Jordan, and Madonna. The U.S. TV blockbuster *Dallas* was, in reruns, the most popular television show in southern China.

Table 1-1 details some of the changes that have taken place. Despite the tight political control symbolized by the 1989 Tiananmen Square crackdown, the Chinese are enjoying a certain degree of personal and economic freedom never seen in their four-thousand-year history. In short, Deng Xiaoping produced an economic miracle in China. Despite his undemocratic rule, he skillfully turned China around and set it on course toward modernization.

Although we believe that China will continue its economic reform, it also has some unique political and economic risks that will affect the returns of global investors. The growing economic disparity between Chinese farmers and city dwellers may cause social unrest. Unchecked corruption could seriously deter foreign investment. The human rights issue may affect China's economic relationship with the West. Moreover, any heavy-handed approach to Hong Kong or Taiwan could also cause major instability in the region.

While China's problems undoubtedly create much uncertainty, and thus risk for investors, the country is simply too big to be ignored. Its economy is close to being the second largest in the world and is projected by the U.S. Central Intelligence Agency (CIA) and the World Bank to reach $20 trillion by 2020. This would make China's output larger than that of the United States in less than 25 years. While these projections may be overly ebullient, and while China's economic growth is likely to slow, it is still probable that growth will continue on a scale unknown throughout history.

TABLE 1-1

Socioeconomic Changes, 1976–1996

	1976	*1996*
Where leaders' children were educated	University of Moscow (Chairman Mao's son)	Drexel University (Jiang Zemin's son)
Political indoctrination	Several times a week	Almost none; people are too busy making money
Private ownership	Not allowed	Encouraged
Popular clothing	Blue or gray Mao jacket	Polo shirts, Levi Strauss jeans
Cosmetics	How dare you wear them!	Avon, Revlon, Lancôme Paris
Power lunch	Fried rice	Big Mac
Blockbuster movie	*Shining Red Star*	*The Lion King*
Favorite music	"The East is Red"	Rock 'n' roll, heavy metal
Status drink	Mao Tai	Cognac XO

In 1848, Karl Marx underestimated the dynamism of capitalism and predicted its demise. Current pundits may make a similar mistake by underestimating the pragmatism of today's Chinese Communists. Lester Thurow, the author and a professor at M.I.T., for example, has suggested that both the twentieth-century capitalists and the Chinese leadership understand "that their own long survival depends upon the elimination of revolutionary conditions" by delivering a better life for the majority of the population.

High Fashion in China, 1996

A Symbol of Cultural Change

One hundred forty-eight years after the publication of *The Communist Manifesto*, a former Red Guard turned investment banker (who prefers not to be identified), mocking Marx's famous concluding remarks, wrote of the current economic situation in China:

> The Chinese "communists" disdain to talk about Marxism. They openly admit that economic prosperity can be attained only by the gradual change of all existing social conditions. Let the ruling classes cash in on a capitalist revolution. The people have nothing to lose but their ideology. They have a lot of money to make. CAPITALISTS OF ALL COUNTRIES, INVEST![1]

1. In *The Communist Manifesto*, Marx wrote, "The Communists disdain to conceal their views and aims. They openly declare that their ends can be attained only by the forcible overthrow of all existing social conditions. Let the ruling classes tremble at a Communistic revolution. The proletarians have nothing to lose but their chains. They have a world to win. WORKERS OF ALL COUNTRIES, UNITE!"

One Elephant: India

India, with its huge potential strength but little finesse in executing it, has long been a lumbering elephant on the world economic stage. Despite being the world's largest democracy, it remained mired in a socialist central planning economy well into the early 1990s. This was particularly ironic as China, the world's largest Communist country, openly embraced free-market economic reforms in the 1980s.

India's politicians ignored this development, feeling that their superior democratic system would easily beat China's authoritarian regime both politically and economically. Until 1978, when China's economic reforms were launched, their assumption was correct. Then, with the terms of the race changed, the results changed also. China's capitalism beat India's socialism hands down.

Eager not to lose the economic race to its rival, India started abandoning its socialist economic policies and has taken steps to open up its economy. Progress has been impressive. Subsidies to state-run industries have been cut, foreign investment is flowing in, and economic growth is picking up. With a population of 920 million and a large, well-educated labor force, India certainly has the potential to become an economic power rivaling China and Japan in the twenty-first century.

Prospective investors, however, need to be aware that the road to prosperity in India resembles the country's pothole-strewn dirt roads. The country's explosive population growth can literally absorb all long-term growth, leaving nothing left for investors. At its current 2 percent growth rate, the population is increasing by almost 20 million people a year and will make India the most populous nation in the world in the early twenty-first century. How to provide education and jobs to such a large population will be a great challenge to the economy. In addition, India's arms race with its mortal rival, Pakistan, causes the country to waste billions of dollars in hard currency each year. Powerful special-interest groups, such as labor and state-owned companies, may also slow down the market-reform process.

The good news for world investors is that the Indian government has little choice but to continue its economic reform process. Not only has China been leaping forward toward prosperity, but India's much smaller neighbors, such as Indonesia, Malaysia, and Thailand, have also become quite prosperous by adopting free-market policies. Even the die-hard Communists in Vietnam have begun to open their economy to market reform and foreign investors. India has no time to lose.

The Flamingos: Latin America

Although the countries of Central and South America contain vast natural resources, political instability has long plagued their economic development. Totalitarianism, corruption, and mismanagement have been the rule rather than the exception. After a military coup in 1973 that overthrew a socialist government, Chile became the first country to begin the process of market reform. Since then, it has deregulated its economy, adopted a free-trade policy, and privatized many state-owned enterprises. Today, Chile has the strongest economy in Latin America with steady economic growth, moderate inflation, and rising exports. Moreover, its performance has improved as democracy has begun to replace an authoritarian oligarchy. It is one of the few governments in the world that actually publicizes its performance goals and the achievements of government departments. It is even implementing performance-related pay for civil servants.

Inspired by Chile's economic success, Mexico launched an economic liberalization program in the late 1980s. It lowered its trade barrier with the United States and privatized many state-run enterprises. These changes helped produce a great economic boom in this debt-laden country during the early 1990s. Unfortunately, political instability and financial mismanagement triggered a currency crisis in late 1994, and this greatly set back its economic growth plans. However, a recovery began in 1996 and Mexico's economy is much stronger today than it was in the 1970s and early 1980s. Paradoxically, the Mexican currency crisis had one beneficial effect on the rest of Latin America. Now the cry is "Let's not let short-term borrowing get out of control. We don't want to have Mexico's problems."

Even the two Latin American economic laggards, Brazil and Argentina, appear to be making an economic turnaround. Brazil, the fifth most populated country in the world, was battered during the late 1980s by runaway inflation, swelling foreign debt, and a declining standard of living. Beginning in 1993, however, Brazil has dramatically cut its inflation and has been growing faster than the Latin American average. Argentina has been aggressively privatizing its industry, and despite a recession during the mid-1990s following the Mexican crisis, substantial growth is forecast into the new century. It appears that growth rates in Latin America are likely to accelerate at the turn of the century. Once again, world investors are charmed by the vast continent of flamingos.

And All the Rest: Eastern Europe and Africa

Across the ocean, many eastern European Cinderellas have rid themselves of the heavy boots of central planning and donned the glass slippers of the free market. The Czech Republic, Hungary, and Poland have been the most successful in this economic transition, with rapid output growth and moderate inflation. After its historic presidential election of 1996, Russia is also expected to continue its program of economic reform. As was the case at the beginning of the twentieth century, this land of Peter the Great is holding some promise for daring investors.

Turkey has also made a dramatic turnaround and become an economic example for the Muslim world. Beginning in the 1980s, the economic liberalization policies of the government raised Turkey's per capita output from $1,400 in 1980 to $2,140 in 1995.

Even the African continent has shown signs of heating up. The beginnings of economic growth in Botswana have already attracted investors from all over the world, including a recent $3 million investment by the American investment powerhouse Morgan Stanley. Morgan Stanley has also invested large amounts of money in South Africa as well as in Egypt, Morocco, Zimbabwe, and Ghana.

Consumer Markets in Emerging Nations

It is well known that population growth in emerging markets far exceeds that in the developed economies. As Figure 1-4 indicates, the world's population increases by 9,000 individuals per hour. The developed economies as a whole account for only 5 percent of that increase. Explosive population growth can create severe problems. But there is a positive aspect to robust population growth coupled with strong economic development: first, it provides an increasing supply of labor in developing countries, and second, it creates the basis for a growing consumer market.

It is relatively simple to measure the size of a consumer market: just multiply the bodies (population) by the bucks (average purchasing power). Of course, it is not an easy matter to express the purchasing power of different countries in terms of a single currency, such as the U.S. dollar. Nevertheless, as shown in Table 1-2, Credit Risk International attempted to do just that in 1996. When it had special trouble in estimating average real purchasing power, it offered a range of estimates, as in the case of China and India.

The table shows that the United States is clearly the world's largest consumer market both in aggregate and in terms of the number of individuals with an effective purchasing power of at least $5,000 per year, an amount sufficient to permit purchases other than bare essentials. But many emerging markets also had substantial average purchasing power, and during the mid-1990s they contained large numbers of individuals with a purchasing power greater than $5,000. Clearly, there are already some serious consumer markets outside the developed economies.

The table also estimates the potential size of the market of consumers with at least $5,000 of purchasing power in the year 2020.

FIGURE 1-4

9,000 More People Every Hour

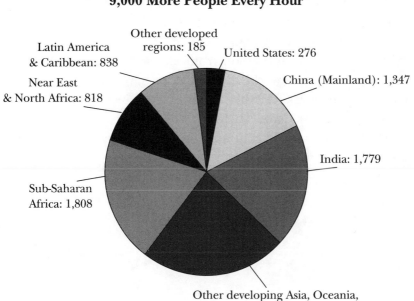

Other developed
regions: 185

Latin America
& Caribbean: 838

United States: 276

China (Mainland): 1,347

Near East
& North Africa: 818

India: 1,779

Sub-Saharan
Africa: 1,808

Other developing Asia, Oceania,
& newly industrialized states: 2,147

SOURCE: U.S. Bureau of the Census, International Data Base

The estimates assume no increase in the proportion of consumers having a purchasing power higher than $5,000. In other words, the proportion of individuals with at least $5,000 of purchasing power in 1994 was applied to the 2020 population figures. By adding the numbers for the developing Asian nations, we can see that the number of Asian consumers with significant purchasing power will substantially exceed that in the United States, *even without a further reduction of the proportion of the population in poverty.* Of course, if Asian consumer markets continue to grow in wealth and prosperity, as we expect, these estimates are likely to understate their size substantially.

It is clear that global demographic trends are decreasing the size of the U.S. consumer market relative to the rest of the world. The locus of buying power is shifting toward the emerging markets. This presents an enormous opportunity not only for multi-national corporations (the current darlings of Wall Street) but for indigenous corporations in emerging markets as well.

As one surveys the vast landscape of emerging markets, there is evidence of a transformation from lands of despair to fields of dreams all over the world. Never before have so many countries chosen a free-market development strategy in their race to economic prosperity. Never before have large consumer markets grown up so rapidly. The hunting grounds for aggressive investors appear to be well stocked.

TABLE 1-2

The Impact of Population Growth on the Growth of World Consumer Markets, 1994 and 2020

	Total Population (in millions) 1994	2020 (projected)	Purchasing Power 1994 Average per Head	Estimated Number of People Having a Purchasing Power Higher than $5,000 (in millions) 1994	2020 (projected)
Developed Countries					
France	58	61	$19,820	53	56
Germany	81	89	19,890	76	84
United Kingdom	58	59	18,870	51	52
United States	261	326	25,860	240	300
Emerging Markets					
Europe:					
Turkey	61	86	4,610	17	24
Poland	38	41	5,380	12	13
Russia	148	150	5,260	55	95
Developing Asia:					
China	1,191	1,438	1,800–2,500	95–148	115–179
India	914	1,290	1,300–1,750	32–41	45–58
Indonesia	190	276	3,690	30	44
Pakistan	126	199	2,210	9	14
Philippines	66	113	2,800	9	16
Thailand	59	69	6,870	28	33
South Korea	45	54	10,940	33	39
Malaysia	20	30	8,610	11	16
Total Developing Asia	2,611	3,469		247–309	322–399
Latin America:					
Brazil	161	194	5,630	52	62
Mexico	92	136	7,050	41	61
Colombia	36	49	5,970	13	18
Argentina	31	43	8,920	16	22
Venezuela	21	31	7,890	12	17
Chile	14	18	9,060	7	9
Africa and the Middle East:					
Nigeria	102	205	1,430	5	10
Egypt	58	92	3,610	10	17
Algeria	27	45	4,390	8	13
Morocco	27	45	3,440	7	11

SOURCES: *World Bank Atlas;* Credit Risk International; U.S. Bureau of the Census.

CHAPTER TWO

The Price Is Right
on the Other Side

SUCCESSFUL INVESTMENT DECISIONS in the stock market have two important elements. First, the companies in which you invest need to produce substantial growth. And we believe that emerging markets now provide the most exciting growth prospects in the world. This fact does not, however, rule out investment mistakes. You can always lose money if you pay too much for your purchases, and you can even do so if you buy a stock that doubles its earnings. Suppose, for example, you pay 100 times earnings for the initial stock purchase and that earnings per share double as anticipated. Does this mean the stock price doubles as well? Almost certainly not. Indeed, after such a dramatic earnings spurt, prospects for future growth will moderate and the earnings multiple will often decline, say to 25. If so, you would lose half your original investment. So before you send your money overseas, you need to ensure that the second element of successful investing is met: be sure that your purchases are made at bargain prices.

Throughout the 1980s and most of the 1990s, the stock markets in most of the developed world have been booming. As stock prices have soared, especially in the United States, bargain hunters have been given a golden shopping opportunity in emerging markets. Relative to stock markets in the developed world, stocks of several emerging markets have rarely been so cheap. That is why we believe many emerging markets offer the best bargains available for the investing public.

Stocks in Emerging Markets Are Bargains

The standard measure used by financial analysts to determine whether a common stock is reasonably priced is a ratio rather than the absolute price of the stock. It is called the price-earnings (P/E) ratio. If IBM, for example, sells at $80 per share, this tells you nothing about how it is valued in the market. Only when we compare IBM's stock price with its earnings per share can we get a sense of its valuation. P/E ratios also create a mechanism for comparing the value of one company with another and one national market with another. For example, if IBM's earnings are $5 per share, we can calculate its P/E ratio as 16 (80 ÷ 5). The P/E ratio allows us to compare IBM with other U.S. companies as well as with Japanese computer makers, such as Fujitsu and Hitachi, and with emerging-market companies, such as Korea's Samsung. Such a broad, overall comparison shows that common stocks in emerging countries tend to sell at lower multiples of company earnings and at lower prices relative to the value of the assets owned by the corporations. In short, some of the most attractive growth companies in the world are available at bargain prices.

As with all measures, however, the P/E ratio is not perfect. Peter Lynch, one of the few investment professionals who deserves a place in the "Portfolio Managers' Hall of Fame," devised a very simple, but quite successful, refinement and used it to locate undervalued stocks. His measure took predicted growth into account. He recognized that stocks with high growth rates tend to sell at high P/E ratios. It stands to reason that if two stocks have the same earnings but one is expected to grow much faster than the other, this one would fetch a higher price. After all, in a few years the faster-growth stock would have the higher earnings. Lynch spent his career attempting to find stocks that promised to deliver high long-term growth yet had relatively low P/E ratios. The ratio of a stock's expected long-term growth rate to its P/E ratio is Lynch's measure of value.

Suppose, for example, that IBM and Intel had the same P/E ratio of 16 times earnings. If IBM were expected to have a long-term growth rate of 8 percent per year, the ratio of growth to the P/E ratio would be 8/16, or 0.5. Let's say that Intel, on the other hand, has an expected growth rate of 16 percent per year. Its growth-to-P/E ratio is thus 16/16, or 1. According to Lynch, Intel would be the better buy because it has a higher growth-to-P/E ratio.

The beauty of buying stocks with high potential growth ratios at low P/E ratios is that as the growth is actually realized, the P/E ratio may rise. As investors become more confident of the growth, stocks are often rewarded with higher ratios. On the other hand, "growth stocks" at very high ratios present substantial risks. Suppose, for example, that in a particular period, growth is not achieved and earnings actually fall. Investors are likely to be hit with a double whammy: the price of the stock is likely to fall even more sharply than the earnings, as the P/E ratio will also shrink. Thus, stocks with high growth-to-P/E ratios offer both greater rewards and less risk.

We think so highly of Lynch's measure that we used it to judge valuation relationships in emerging markets relative to developed ones. The results show that growth-to-P/E ratios tend to be higher in emerging markets and clearly support our thesis that bargain hunters need to look beyond the stock markets in the developed world.

We started our analysis with forty-six relatively large firms in emerging markets. Their growth rates were obtained from the International Brokerage Evaluation Service (IBES). This organization collects five-year growth projections made by financial analysts for different companies and averages them to give a composite projection for each company studied. The P/E ratios were more easily obtained. We simply divided the stock prices of the forty-six firms by their earnings per share. We then picked a sample of forty-six similar firms in developed markets and obtained the same data. Each emerging-market firm was coupled with a developed-market firm located in the same business and industry. For example, AT&T in the United States (10 percent expected growth, P/E ratio of 24) was coupled with Telecom Argentina (13 percent expected growth, P/E ratio of 13). Figure 2-1 presents the results of our analysis, showing that growth-to-P/E ratios tend to be considerably higher in emerging markets. Emerging-market stocks tend to have higher growth rates and lower P/E ratios. Investors seeking the best values will have to look beyond their local stock markets to find the best bargains for the twenty-first century.

In another analysis, we compared entire markets rather than comparable companies. This comparison is shown in Figure 2-2. Here the average P/E ratio is calculated for each national market index. The growth rate is the projected five-year growth rate of each country's GDP. Since corporate earnings and the GDP tend to move together, the GDP growth rate is a good proxy for real earnings growth (growth net of inflation). On the Lynch measure of value, emerging markets again win hands down over the developed stock markets. That is, growth can be purchased at a far lower price in emerging markets than it can be bought in the United States and western Europe.

Another valuation measure also suggests the attractiveness of emerging markets. One compares the price of a company's stock with the value of the assets it owns. Thus, if a stock sells at a price per share of $20 and has assets per share (on its accounting books) of $16, the stock is said to have a price-to-book-value (P/BV) ratio of 1.25 ($20/$16). It turns out that this ratio has proved somewhat successful in predicting differences in security returns in the United States. Equities that sell at low prices relative to their book values have tended to produce superior performance. Of course, one should maintain some degree of skepticism that this relationship will continue to be reliable since recent waves of downsizing and plant write-offs have made book value an unreliable guide to the true worth of a firm's assets. Nonetheless, the P/BV ratio remains a crude and still somewhat useful guide to value.

The investment firm of Smith Barney found that the P/E and P/BV ratios were both useful in predicting differential returns in emerging markets. The P/BV results are shown in Figure 2-3. Note from the figure that, at least for some periods in the past,

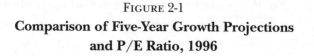

FIGURE 2-1

Comparison of Five-Year Growth Projections and P/E Ratio, 1996

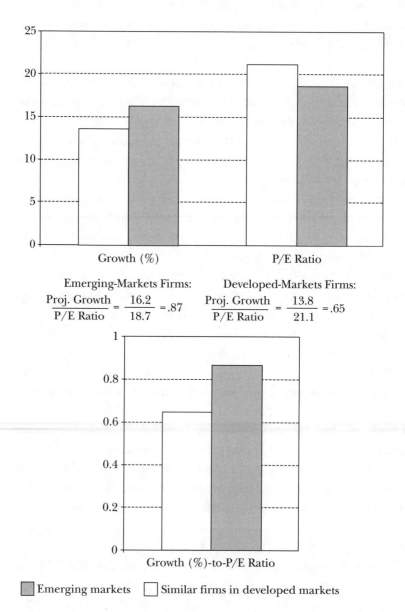

Emerging-Markets Firms:

$$\frac{\text{Proj. Growth}}{\text{P/E Ratio}} = \frac{16.2}{18.7} = .87$$

Developed-Markets Firms:

$$\frac{\text{Proj. Growth}}{\text{P/E Ratio}} = \frac{13.8}{21.1} = .65$$

Growth (%)-to-P/E Ratio

■ Emerging markets   □ Similar firms in developed markets

FIGURE 2-2
Valuation Ratios in Different National Markets, 1997

Growth-to-P/E Ratios (Higher Ratios Represent Better Value)

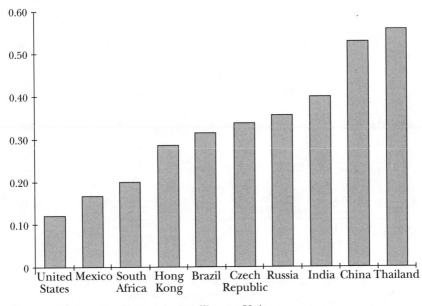

SOURCES: Datastream, Economist Intelligence Unit.

there has been a good deal of predictability of stock returns from
different emerging markets based upon the average P/BV ratio at
the beginning of the period. When stocks could be bought at low
P/BV ratios (as well as low P/E ratios), they tended to produce
relatively high subsequent returns, as was the case for Argentina.
On the other hand, when stocks in national markets tended to sell
at very high P/BV ratios (for example, in Taiwan), subsequent returns tended to be very low. However, given the extremely wide
differences in accounting practices among nations, it would not
be wise to put complete reliance on any single valuation factor.
Nevertheless, the closeness of the correlations of returns with the
P/BV and P/E ratios, plus the fact that such ratios in emerging
markets tend to be lower than in developed markets, add a powerful argument that global bargain hunters need to be aware of
the values that exist in emerging stock markets.

FIGURE 2-3

Relationship of Price-to-Book-Value as of January 1989 and Subsequent Eight-Year Returns, 1989–1996

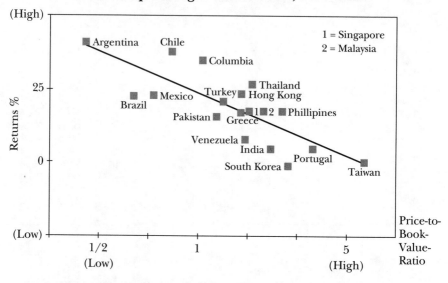

On average, emerging markets whose stocks had low P/BV ratios at the start of 1989 brought home higher returns over the subsequent eight-year period than emerging markets whose stocks had higher-than-average P/BV ratios.

SOURCE: Smith Barney & Company, *Global Asset Allocation Report.*

A whole panoply of ratios and indicators show the values that exist in the rapidly developing parts of the world and the tendency of attractively priced stocks to generate very high returns. Today, the world's securities markets are like a huge shopping bazaar, and the real bargains are usually not found close to home. In our increasingly global economy, many of the "home run" investments of the future will be found by expanding one's horizons well beyond national borders.

The Home-Country Bias and the Likely Future Flows of Funds into Emerging Markets

During the mid-1990s, despite the very attractive opportunities that were available for investors who broadened their portfolios to include emerging markets, U.S. institutional investors held close to 95 percent of their equity funds in domestic stocks. This tendency of investors to eschew foreign markets is known in the finance profession as "the home-country bias," and it is not peculiar to the United States. It is characteristic of all the developed nations of the world. For example, France, a nation that considers itself the heart and soul of Europe, also exhibits a strong proclivity to stick close to home, especially considering its small relative size. During the mid-1990s, French institutional investors held 92 percent of their funds in French companies despite the fact that the market value of all French company common stocks is only about 3 percent of the world total. Similarly, Japanese investors overwhelmingly concentrate on Japan, German investors on Germany, and so forth. Fund managers in all the developed nations tend to take a very parochial view of investment alternatives.

There are signs, however, that this situation is changing, especially in the U.S. investment community. As of early 1997, the great majority of large institutional investors (such as those managing the big corporate and state pension funds) indicated that their goal is to increase their portfolios' share of non-U.S. stocks to 10 percent or even higher. Even 10 percent would be far below the approximately two-thirds share of non-U.S. stocks in the total market value of the world's stock markets. Suppose that U.S. investors decide to bring their share of foreign stocks to only 7 or 8 percent of their total assets and that emerging-market investments comprise 20 percent of the foreign total. Working through the arithmetic of such an exercise has important implications for world securities markets. It suggests that the flow of funds going into emerging markets will more than double over the investment flows during the first half of the 1990s. Anything close to this will provide a major boost for emerging stock markets into the twenty-first century.

Certainly, a major reason for the home-country bias is a lack of information about foreign investing (an information gap we hope this book will at least partially close). There is also a tendency for investors to demand excessive risk premiums for foreign investments despite the fact that such investments can actually reduce, rather than increase, risk. We believe that as more information is made available and emerging nations, with their large requirements to raise funds for infrastructure, reduce investment barriers and take further measures to make investing in their countries easier, the home-country bias will tend to decline. In fact, the proportion of U.S. funds invested abroad has been increasing for at least a decade. If we are correct that further understanding of our global marketplace will encourage even larger flows of funds in the future, we can see an additional attraction to investing now. If even a small fraction of fund managers in developed nations increase their purchases of emerging-market stocks, the resulting flow of investment funds will serve as a cushion for these stock prices during declining markets and a spur to greater capital appreciation when the markets rise.

Four Fundamental Reasons Why Rapid Growth Will Continue

There is, of course, a "castle-in-the-air" quality about relying on the growth projections of financial analysts. As Samuel Goldwyn is reported to have said, forecasts are notoriously difficult to make—especially about the future. We are only too aware that financial charts can be churned out to support almost any view. Thus, there is more—much more—than P/E and P/BV ratios underlying our belief that emerging markets represent extraordinary value for savvy investors. Emerging-market economies, as a whole, will grow far more rapidly than those in the developed world for many years to come, for four fundamental reasons: (1) Throughout the developing world, centralized control has been replaced by the liberating influence of free markets; (2) low labor costs, strong work ethics, and reasonably high literacy rates will allow many developing countries to create strongly competitive positions in world markets; (3) open trading systems and the ability to transfer technology and capital will give emerging-market economies the tools they need to develop rapidly; (4) high savings rates will augment the flow of foreign capital to emerging markets, enabling them to undertake the large investments required in infrastructure and business without severe constraints.

Economic Freedom Is Everywhere

Sometimes the retelling of old fables can help explain major changes in the world's political geography, such as the move from Marx to markets.

Once upon a time, there was a little red hen who scratched about the barnyard until she uncovered some grains of wheat. She called her neighbors and said, "If we plant this wheat, we shall have bread to eat. Who will help me plant it?"

"Not I," said the cow.

"Not I," said the duck.

"Not I," said the pig.

"Not I," said the goose.

"Then I will," said the little red hen. And she did. The wheat grew tall and ripened into golden grain. "Who will help me reap my wheat?" asked the little red hen.

"Not I," said the duck and the pig and the cow and the goose.

"Then I will," said the little red hen. And she did.

At last it came time to bake the bread. "Who will help me bake the bread?" asked the little red hen.

"No way," said the others.

So she baked five loaves herself and held them up for her neighbors to see.

They all wanted some and, in fact, demanded a share. But the little red hen said, "No, I can eat the five loaves myself."

"Obscene profits!" cried the cow.

"Capitalist exploiter!" screamed the duck.

"To each according to his need!" yelled the goose and the pig.

Then a government agent and party official came and said to the little red hen, "You must not be greedy—you must divide the fruits of your labor with the idle."

And they lived happily ever after, including the little red hen, who smiled and clucked, "I am grateful. I am grateful."

But her neighbors wondered why she never again baked any more bread.

A major study, *Index of Economic Freedom,* provides convincing evidence that free markets are far more effective than government control in promoting growth. The study showed that between 1980 and 1993, countries with economic freedom enjoyed a 2.9 percent real annual growth rate in per capita income, while countries without free markets had a 1.4 percent *decrease* in income per person. No matter where your travels take you today, from Brazil to Bangladesh, the invisible hand of the market economy has split the rusted shackles of central planning and collectivization. As a result, stock markets now flourish from Shanghai to Santiago. The stage has been set for enormous growth, and vast regions of the world should soon enjoy much higher standards of living.

The end of communism has created a major reversal in the world's economic structure as nations throughout Asia, South America, and Africa have been selling off their state-owned enterprises. Even in mainland China, which on paper remains a socialist country, the Central Committee of the Communist Party declared in 1992 that henceforth China would be a market economy. Three-quarters of the nation's output is now produced by profit-seeking units, and more than 90 percent of the prices charged for goods and services are subject to the laws of supply and demand. China's younger generation now worships Madonna, the material girl, rather than Lei Feng, the puritan soldier who devoted his life to communism. Becoming rich is China's national economic goal.

During the period of collectivized agriculture in the People's

Republic of China, output growth ranged between 2 and 3 percent. Following decollectivization, the growth of agricultural output exploded at an 8 to 9 percent rate, despite a slower rate of growth of the labor force. The diet of the Chinese population has thus changed dramatically. In Chile, after years of stagnation under both socialism and a brutal military dictatorship, democracy was peacefully restored in 1990. Since then, the economy has flourished, per capita income has boomed, and almost everything, including public housing and social security, has been privatized. Even the national currency has been outsourced to a private printing company.

In eastern Europe and Latin America, governments have been unloading steel mills, phone companies, oil fields, and banks. Under government control, YPF, the Argentine oil company, was an inefficient enterprise losing billions of dollars a year and near bankruptcy. Today, it is one of the best-run and most profitable oil companies in the world. Deregulation has been a worldwide phenomenon, even in countries where the heavy hand of bureaucracy had severely restricted economic activity. For example, reforms in India began in 1991, freeing the country's economy from regulations that had hobbled it for decades. Countries such as Argentina, Brazil, Malaysia, Pakistan, and Turkey allow foreign investors virtually unrestricted access to their stock markets. The lessons are clear throughout the world: central planning stultifies growth, and a combination of free markets and individual initiative can put any country onto the road to development, high employment, and affluence. Karl Marx must be doing somersaults in his grave.

The People Are Smart and Thrifty

Perhaps the greatest natural resource that many emerging markets possess is a well-educated and motivated workforce that is willing to work hard to reach the high standards of living in the developed world. As Nobel Laureate Sir W. Arthur Lewis concluded, in a personal conversation with the author shortly before his death:

I have devoted a lifetime to the study of developing economies. I have examined strategies for development, the role of foreign trade, of savings and investment, the most helpful role of government, and a myriad of other factors. I am now convinced that nothing matters more than the work ethic and entrepreneurial spirit of the population.

People's capacity for work in many emerging markets, especially in Asia, is nothing short of remarkable. The diligence and determination of South Korean workers, for example, make even the Japanese worker seem like a shirker. During South Korea's recent rapid-growth phase, the workweek approached sixty hours. In construction projects in the Middle East, South Korean workers were without rivals in their willingness to work long hours in a scorching climate. Labor costs are low and like other Asians, Koreans are preoccupied with education. Unable to make simple batteries during the 1960s, South Korea in the late 1990s has become a leading manufacturer of sophisticated computer chips. The World Bank in its study of what it called "the East Asian miracle" concluded, "people in these countries have simply studied harder and worked harder than people in other countries." Moreover, the diaspora of some 60 million overseas Chinese with their entrepreneurial and intensely commercial culture has energized the entire Pacific Rim region. Overseas Chinese share an abiding belief in hard work and education. These are not musty relics from the culture's past but compelling rules to live by.

An abundant pool of cheap, well-educated labor is available from Russia and eastern European countries all the way to East Asia. Literacy rates in the Four Tigers, the Tiger Cubs, and many countries in Latin America approach the rates in the United States. Children in many emerging markets spend far more time in school and doing homework than the typical child in the United States.

For highly skilled labor, such as computer programming, the Internet provides the global telecommunications link allowing the developed world to access programming skills. Today, Bangalore, in India, has seven software development parks with over 5 million workers and is one of the world's largest exporters of computer software via the Internet. Passengers traveling by American Airlines or SwissAir have software companies in India to thank for the fact that their aircraft run on time. The London Underground runs on Indian computer programs—as do bank accounts at Citibank and credit card records at American Express. Similar high-tech software development parks are now springing up in Beijing and Shanghai.

Table 2-1 presents estimates of average labor costs for selected countries in the developed and developing world. The differences are remarkable. Average labor costs in the United States are some sixty times greater than in China. The authors of the book *China Wakes* asked a Communist district party secretary in Dongguan whether a minimum wage might be a good idea for China. The response might have come from the editorial page of *The Wall Street Journal:* "What's the point of a minimum wage?" the party secretary replied, lifting his eyebrows. "If both sides want to work for a given wage, why should we interfere?"

China may have one of the most flexible labor markets in the world. Multinational corporations may wonder with good reason why they should pay an American high school graduate $15,000 a year when they can hire a better-educated Chinese graduate for $100 a month—or why a third-rate American physicist should be hired at $75,000 a year when a Nobel Prize winner in the former Soviet Union can be hired for $250 a month. A German business executive, considering the vast labor pools in the former Communist countries to the east, remarked, "It's like a shot of adrenaline to be in Berlin and realize that one hour away by car, in a country where you no longer need a visa to travel, labor costs are only five to ten percent of what they are in Germany." Small wonder that the growth prospects in many emerging markets appear so attractive.

TABLE 2-1
World Labor Costs per Hour, Manufacturing Sector

	1995 Cost
Germany	$31.88
Japan	23.66
France	19.34
United States	17.20
Italy	16.48
Canada	16.03
Australia	14.40
Britain	13.77
Spain	12.70
South Korea	7.40
Singapore	7.28
Taiwan	5.82
Hong Kong	4.82
Brazil	4.28
Chile	3.63
Poland	2.09
Hungary	1.70
Argentina	1.67
Malaysia	1.59
Mexico	1.51
Czech Republic	1.30
Philippines	0.71
Russia	0.60
Thailand	0.46
Indonesia	0.30
China	0.25
India	0.25

SOURCE: Morgan Stanley Research.

High Technology Has Already Arrived

At the beginning of the 1990s, a China Products Fair would bring a wry smile to the faces of browsing foreign traders. A story in the *Nikkei Weekly* described these products as "the clunky toaster; the cheesy-looking welder; a tank-sized refrigerator looking as if it belonged at the head of a May Day parade. At best functional, always 20 years out of date, Chinese products were destined almost exclusively for Third World markets." Today, international market analysts are convinced that, by the turn of the century, China will export many consumer and industrial products equal in quality to those from Japan. The turnaround has been made possible by technology transfer. The heart of China's industrial policy has been acquiring foreign technology. By the mid-1990s, Chinese companies signed approximately six thousand technology transfer agreements with developed nations worth nearly $50 billion.

From low to high tech, the tools and technology to make everything from screwdrivers to semiconductors can be transferred to foreign countries. In a global economy, profit can be realized by cross-border transfers of technology into countries with cheap, well-trained labor with a strong work ethic. The Stanley Works has transferred its production of hammers and screwdrivers from Connecticut to Thailand. Philips has transferred television manufacturing from Holland to Taiwan. General Electric, Zenith, Texas Instruments, Hitachi, and Siemens have formed joint ventures with South Korea. Motorola and Hewlett-Packard not only manufacture pagers and computer keyboards in Singapore but have now even transferred some of their research and development facilities there. Asia, with its young and receptive population, has been the main beneficiary of technology transfer and has recently been successful in luring expatriate engineers and scientists back home. Technology transfers have also taken place in Latin America, eastern Europe, and other parts of the developing world.

The Financial Undergrowth Is Impressive

Rapid growth requires large investments, not only in business, plant, and equipment but also in infrastructure, such as telecommunications, roads, electric power, and so on. Capital to finance these investments can be obtained internally from national savings or imported either through direct foreign investment by multinational corporations or through the sale of securities to foreigners. Reliance on foreign capital, however, especially short-term borrowing, creates its own hazards. Such reliance can be hazardous, as Mexico discovered in the early 1990s, when short-term capital flows from abroad stopped abruptly at the first sign of Mexican political instability.

The good news is that stable internal sources of capital are available for many developing countries. Asian countries are particularly fortunate in having some of the highest savings rates in the world. During the 1990s, savings rates as a percentage of national income have exceeded one-third in China, South Korea, Indonesia, and Singapore and have been close to a third in Hong Kong, Taiwan, and India. For comparison, total savings in the United States is a scant 15 percent of national income. The simple fact is that in many emerging markets, people not only work harder but also save more, allowing them to accumulate physical capital. And they study harder, permitting them to build what economists call "human capital."

Moreover, countries in almost every part of the Third World (including eastern Europe and the former Soviet Union) have been undergoing a revolution in economic policy making. In macroeconomic policy, budget deficits are being brought under better control and great efforts have been made to curb chronically high inflation. Further, the move toward more free market–oriented economic policies has made developing countries far more attractive as potential recipients of foreign capital. Thus, everything needed for growth is finally coming together. Technology and capital from the developed world are merging with a massive labor pool and, in many cases, abundant natural resources.

Skeptics may well point out that we have held high hopes for development in the past, only to see them dissolve into bitter disappointment after a cycle of excessive borrowing, a Third World debt crisis, and economic collapse. It is always extraordinarily dangerous to say that "this time is different," but in fact the late 1990s are not like the late 1970s. Not only are there systemic improvements in government finance, monetary control, and deregulation of markets, but even the character of foreign investment has changed.

Unlike the situation in the 1980s when most of the flow of funds to emerging markets took the form of short-term lending, the financing flows of the mid- to late 1990s have primarily represented permanent capital. Debt financing is more likely to be in the form of long-term bonds than short-term borrowing. Equity finance is far more important than before, and the volume of direct foreign investment in factories and machines by multinational corporations has seen a tenfold increase from the mid-1980s to the mid-1990s. Moreover, investments flowing to emerging markets are less from banks to governments and state-owned enterprises and more from capital markets and multinational corporations to private firms. By 1996, worldwide foreign direct investment in emerging markets totaled approximately $500 billion. There are good reasons to expect that movements toward free markets and the changes noted in external finance will reinforce each other, forming a virtuous circle.

Could We Be Wrong?

Could economic euphoria about the growth prospects of the emerging markets turn into bitter disappointment, as has sometimes been the case in the past? Undoubtedly, there will be disappointments, and the cycle of excessive optimism, heavy borrowing, and economic collapse that occurred in Mexico in the early 1990s could well be repeated in some countries. Moreover, critics, such as Paul Krugman, a professor of economics at M.I.T., correctly point out that eventually the dismal economic law of diminishing returns will set in, and that without significant improvements in overall productivity, the recent high growth rates of emerging markets will tend to fall. But even the most pessimistic analysts cannot help but conclude that growth rates in the poor countries that have begun the process of development will continue to be considerably larger than those in the developed world.

For one thing, there is still an enormous pool of unused or underutilized labor available in most emerging markets. For instance, an average U.S. worker is equipped with $50,000 of capital. An average worker in India, on the other hand, has less than $2,000 of capital with which to work. An additional $2,000 of capital to the U.S. worker is like an extra dessert after a full meal—satisfying but not essential. The same amount of capital to the Indian worker, however, is more like food for a starving child. Coupled with a transfer of modern technology and a hardworking labor force, capital investments can significantly improve productivity in emerging markets such as India. Moreover, the resulting high rate of return to capital would be unattainable in a well-capitalized developed economy. Because of the huge differences in capital endowments, emerging markets will take a very long time to reach the developed countries' level of capitalization. As a result, growth rates and the rate of return on capital in emerging markets are likely to remain high for many years to come.

In conclusion, as we broadly survey the vast landscape of emerging markets, simultaneous revolutions in economics, communications, politics, and technology promise to create an environment that will sustain rapid growth for the developing world well into the twenty-first century. Signs of monumental change are all around us. We are not simply entering a new century; we are entering a new era.

PART I HIGHLIGHTS:

1. Rapid economic growth and low-priced securities make emerging markets among the best investment bargains in the world.

2. Emerging markets are likely to sustain robust growth due to four powerful economic engines:

   a. Free markets provide strong incentive for entrepreneurs.
   b. An educated, low-cost labor pool with a strong work ethic provides a competitive edge.
   c. Modern technology is easily transferred from the developed to the developing world.
   d. Domestic and foreign capital will fuel the rapid growth of many emerging markets.

3. Emerging-market securities are significantly underrepresented in both institutional and individual portfolios. Even a small increase in investment flows to these markets will provide a major boost for stock prices.

PART II

THE DANGERS
TO BE AVOIDED

AT THE TURN of the twentieth century, a tidal wave of globalization washed over the world. Unfortunately, most investors surfing on this wave were thoroughly doused by the sinking of many of the emerging markets for long periods of time. They were the lucky ones, for other investors drowned, their assets totally underwater to this day. As we now ride the second wave of globalization at the start of the twenty-first century, we need to ask: Will investors in emerging markets fare better this time?

We believe the answer is "yes," that this time is really different. We base our optimism on the fundamental geopolitical changes that have taken place in the world. While defaults may still occur and entire markets may still sink, the following three profound socioeconomic changes of the past century have important positive implications for investors.

First, the risk of nationalization and government expropriation has been greatly reduced with the apparent death of communism as a valid economic philosophy. Throughout Asia, Europe, and even Africa, countries are reeling from the disastrous effects of planned economies, systems that promoted neither economic growth nor the welfare of their people. While progress toward free markets will not be continuous, we do not expect Russia, or any other country, to reverse their recent economic reforms and return to a planned economic system.

BRUCE BEATTIE
Courtesy Daytona Beach News-Journal

Second, tensions among developed countries and between developed and developing nations have been reduced with the passing of colonialism. In 1910, emerging markets were known as "colonies" and were the political and economic fiefdoms of major powers. The deep resentment of subjected peoples to the rule of, and exploitation by, foreign powers created major risks for colonial investors. While turn-of-the-century colonizers used battleships to help guarantee their returns, today's investors rely on the self-interest of developing countries. These nations have enormous capital needs for infrastructure and continued growth, and only the major developed countries can supply such cash infusions. Leaders throughout emerging markets have a vested interest in seeing that their political systems ensure a stable investment environment.

Finally, there is the maturation of the capitalistic philosophy. It has, if you will, evolved into a kinder and gentler system, one that now ameliorates some of the destabilizing political tensions previously associated with free markets. Nineteenth-century capitalism was rife with ugly features, such as child labor, the opium trade, and slave markets. It also created huge income gaps between the "haves" and the "have-nots," excesses that often led to social unrest and revolution. While many of the same problems remain today—not only in the United States but throughout the world—most countries have some sort of social insurance system that provides something of a safety net for the poorest individuals. While these systems are usually quite rudimentary in most emerging-market nations, they can partially alleviate the pain that is frequently associated with the transition from a planned to a competitive economy.

Of course, not all is perfect in the world at the beginning of the third millennium. Yes, it is possible to dream of billions of Chinese and Indians diligently producing goods and services for the world at large and, in the process, becoming wealthy enough to purchase all manner of food, clothing, television sets, communications equipment, financial services, and automobiles. That vision increases the heartbeat of any red-blooded investor—including ours. New problems, however, have risen as others have faded away. The relative political order imposed by colonial powers has given way to unstable political situations in many countries. This lack of stability is further aggravated by weak legal systems and the accompanying pervasiveness of corruption, weak accounting standards, unethical business behavior, and markets constrained by tight liquidity and high transactions costs. While these factors may be ameliorated as emerging markets develop, they have nevertheless created an investment situation rife with consistent volatility.

Looming over all are the three long-term portents of worldwide doom: overpopulation, environmental pollution, and the rise of nationalism. While population growth can provide enormous opportunities for emerging markets by providing an increased supply of workers and a growing consumer market, unchecked population growth can create hurdles to world stability. The world had only 1.8 billion people in 1914. Thirty years from now, it will bulge with almost 8 billion. This teeming mass of humanity, imbued with the desire to emulate consumption standards in developed countries, will impose enormous burdens on the world's environment and natural resources. The world's wool supply, for example, could be exhausted if every individual living in China today had only one pair of wool socks. Imagine what would happen to oil prices and air pollution if every Chinese and Indian family owned a car! The fight to control scarce resources could cause intractable regional conflicts, and, fueled by nationalism, these conflicts could be deadly for world political stability.

There is little any investor can do to counteract the effects of these three long-term factors. Pessimists take inordinate comfort in the fact that if they combine to overwhelm emerging markets, they will also ultimately destroy or seriously weaken the material well-being of all developed nations as well. We, however, are optimists. While we will detail some of the obvious and hidden dangers of investing in emerging markets, we believe there are ways to mitigate these risks, and that the odds of success for investors are quite good.

CHAPTER THREE

Political Instability Can Sour Many an Investment Opportunity

THOSE SEEKING INVESTMENT riches in emerging countries often find political instability lurking around many a corner. Indeed, this may well be the greatest hazard they will encounter. It is not a new hazard, however, for it is one that has long plagued investors. More than a hundred years ago, people in western Europe had already invested substantial amounts of capital in the then-emerging economies of Argentina, Mexico, China, India, Russia, South Africa, and the United States. Some economies completely submerged as a result of wars and revolutions, causing investors to suffer huge financial losses. Today, as we begin a new wave of emerging-market investment, it is natural to ask: What can we learn from past experience? Is it possible to design strategies to minimize the risks of emerging-market investment? A review of investors' experience in emerging markets at the start of the twentieth century will serve as a useful background.

Playing Russian Investment Roulette

Unlike other European countries, Russia was a backward agricultural society at the end of the seventeenth century. But change was in the air—or rather, on the road. In 1697, a tall, handsome Russian carpenter went to work in a Dutch shipyard in Zaandam. After a long day of sweaty labor, he would return to his small hut and read everything from history to medicine, and most of all, books about manufacturing, the kind of material read by today's MBAs.

This remarkable carpenter was none other than Peter the Great, who ascended to the throne of the Russian Empire at age seventeen. Determined to transform his backward nation into a modern European power, he toured Europe incognito. Upon returning to his country, he launched a series of reforms to westernize Russia. To speed up the process, he lured nine hundred artists, craftsmen, and technical experts to Russia. Later he also sent young Russians abroad to learn Western crafts and trades. He established hospitals, built schools, and published scientific books. In order to force his people to make a clean break from the past, he even imposed fines for wearing oriental dress and growing beards. These reforms greatly sped up Russia's modernization. By the turn of the twentieth century, the country had been transformed from a weak state into a powerful empire.

To this day, the vastness of Russia's territory (roughly equal to that of the United States and China put together) and the richness of its natural resources remain unmatched by any other country in the world. At the turn of the twentieth century, it also enjoyed another great advantage: its labor costs were significantly below those of the industrialized nations. With a population more than 50 percent greater than that of the United States, it was clearly the largest emerging market of its time.

The Industrial Revolution and foreign investment further accelerated Russia's development. Industrial production doubled during the 1890s, then doubled again during the first decade of the 1900s. Productivity growth was especially impressive compared with the standards of the time. With increasing use of new technology, such as steam engines, Russia achieved a 75 percent increase in production with only a 27 percent increase in the workforce during the 1897–1908 period. Russia had the best steel production technology in Europe in 1914. It also ran an enormous trade surplus, and inflation was almost nonexistent.

Foreign money poured into Russia, much of it coming from the

European and American bankers arriving first class on ocean liners or railways. Impressed by St. Petersburg's elegant European buildings, beautiful Russian women wearing French perfumes, and the high cultural sophistication represented by the Russian ballet, these investment professionals saw unlimited potential.

The Russians obligingly created mechanisms for investors to realize that potential. More than a half-dozen organized securities exchanges boomed in their country. The most active, located in St. Petersburg, boasted a list of 612 securities in 1912. Russian stocks were also listed on the foreign securities exchanges in London, Paris, and Berlin to facilitate trading. Out of the total 5.2 billion rubles of Russian stocks and bonds issued during the 1908–1913 period, roughly a third were sold to foreign investors.

Of the many securities issued, British and French investors especially loved Russian railroad gold bonds, which were secured by Russian government guarantees, payable in gold, and free of currency risk. The eager financiers included many of the most prominent banks in the world, such as Barings and Rothschild of England, Crédit Lyonnais and Société Générale of France, and Citibank (then National City Bank) of the United States. These banks helped finance the construction of a vast railroad transportation network, including the famous 5,786-mile-long Trans-Siberian Railway. The Russian government also sought foreign joint-venture partners for some of its state-owned enterprises. Competition among foreign companies to join these ventures was no less intense than in East Asia today. In 1907, when the Russian armament giant Putilov sought outside capital and technology, the French company Schneider and the German company Krupp fought an extremely nasty seven-year battle to participate. The French company eventually won by enlisting the diplomatic support of its government and by taking advantage of a massive infusion of capital from French banks.

For a while in the early 1900s, everything seemed to be going well in Russia. Unfortunately, this prosperity was built on an active volcano, one topped by the leadership of the willful, autocratic Tsar Nicholas II. Disturbed by Japan's expansion in the Far East, he plunged his ill-prepared country into a disastrous Russo-Japanese war. Badly defeated, unwilling to undertake real political reform, and unable to improve the conditions of many Russian workers, the tsarist government was then dragged into World War I.

Few investors, however, noticed these early signs of looming disaster. In his book *The Global Bankers,* Professor Roy Smith described the mentality of investors at the time:

> Investors saw foreign bonds as an easy way to earn a much higher return on their investments than they could make on comparably rated U.S. bonds. . . . Few had any idea of the resources or the capability of the borrowers to repay the loans or of the social and political conditions in the countries involved.

For these investors, the math was simple. The Russian five-year gold bonds yielded 6.75 percent compared with a yield of approximately 6 percent on Britain's bonds of similar maturity. The extra .75 percent interest appeared to make the risk worthwhile. British and French soldiers confidently purchased Russian bonds for their families before they went off to fight in World War I. Who could imagine that a large country like Russia, with its vast natural resources and huge gold reserves, would ever default on its debt!

History, though, was about to teach investors an expensive lesson. Russia's poorly organized involvement in World War I led to many humiliating defeats. In March 1917, the tsarist government was overthrown. In April, the master politician Lenin seized the opportunity provided by the resulting chaos, and by November he had established the first Communist state in the world. Shortly after taking power, the Soviet government repudiated all international debt obligations and nationalized foreign companies without compensation. This was thrifty internal politics, for at the time Russia owed foreign governments and investors 13.8 billion rubles ($7.1 billion). (Had investors put their money into a 6 percent interest account in the United States, these investments would now be worth $700 billion.)

Acting on the World Investment Stage

The dramatic rise and fall of the Russian market was not an isolated event. It was part of a tidal wave of globalization driven by the rapid expansion of the colonial powers and the Industrial Revolution. Productivity in the industrial nations had increased so much that it was absolutely necessary for them to find new markets and raw materials overseas. The development of railways and steamboats allowed companies to ship goods abroad efficiently. The telegraph permitted worldwide rapid communication. The growth in world trade brought great riches not only to the industrialized nations but also to some of the developing nations, where enormously attractive investment opportunities beckoned.

Britain became the largest supplier of capital to the world. British overseas investment doubled from 1880 to 1900, then doubled again to more than $20 billion in 1914, just before the outbreak of World War I. Billions were invested in the United States as well as in Canada, Argentina, Australia, New Zealand, South Africa, India, and Ceylon. France was the second largest player, with $10 billion of overseas investment in 1914. It was said at the time that out of ten people seated in a French railway carriage, eight owned foreign securities, with seven of those securities being Russian. Germany, a relative latecomer to the game, invested heavily in Turkey, the Balkans, Russia, and Latin America, especially Argentina.

Argentina was among the "hottest" emerging markets at the turn of the century. With an economy that was ranked seventh largest in the world, it appeared to have coequal status with the United States as far as investment potential was concerned. Unfortunately, Argentine politics destroyed that balance. Despite huge capital infusions, decades of military coups, domestic unrest, and market interruptions dragged down the economy. Eighty years later, Argentina remained an emerging market with a per capita output of $7,000 in the early 1990s, about one-third of Hong Kong's $20,000. There was an interesting episode at the turn of the twentieth century when an Argentine debt-underwriting failure caused a liquidity crisis in the famous British bank Barings. Had it not been rescued by the Bank of England, Barings would have gone under a hundred years ago. The cause of that financial crisis was not a rogue trader in Singapore but seemingly prudent bankers in London who lent feverishly to Argentina as if its securities were riskless.

Political instability created some enormous losses for emerging-market investors throughout the twentieth century. The photographic montage on the following page shows some of the now-worthless securities that were once traded in such places as St. Petersburg, Shanghai, Mexico City, Buenos Aires, Budapest, Warsaw, and Santiago. While we believe that history will not repeat itself in precisely the same way in the twenty-first century, we must also acknowledge the dangerous inherent political risk in many developing nations, especially those still emerging from totalitarian rules.

Survivorship Bias

The cases of Russia, Argentina, and other submerged markets illustrate the important point that, despite huge potential and seemingly strong fundamental prerequisites for growth, some countries may fail to emerge and may even submerge, in which case, investors could lose their entire investment. When we looked at the high past returns from many emerging markets in Part I, we did not take this possibility into account. Return data for submerged markets are not available. By using *continuous* price data for emerging markets *currently existing*, the computation implicitly assumes that these markets cannot suffer a complete failure like that of Russia. The calculation thus ignores the historical fact that investments in some markets have become worthless. If we want to use the estimated average emerging-market returns to project future expected returns, we need to take into consideration the possibility that some markets may not survive in the future.

Unfortunately, modern finance has not developed a proper way

Some defaulted bonds from around the world.

of measuring the probability of survival. For instance, what is the probability that Hong Kong's capital market will survive into the twenty-first century now that it has been taken over by China? Is it 95 percent or 80 percent? Many financial economists solve the problem by simply assuming that the probability is 100 percent. Obviously, this is not correct. As a result, any estimates that are computed on the basis of past market performance will overestimate the expected payoffs from emerging markets while seriously underestimating the downside risk of the investments.

To gauge the importance of this survivorship bias, it is useful to know that there existed at least thirty-six securities exchanges at the turn of the century. As pointed out in a recent study by Professor Stephen Brown of New York University and others, "More than half of these suffered at least one major hiatus in trading." They included Amsterdam, Belgrade, Berlin, Brussels, Budapest, Buenos Aires, Cairo, Copenhagen, Frankfurt, Hong Kong, Istanbul, Lisbon, Madrid, Mexico City, Moscow, Prague, Rio de Janeiro, Santiago, Seoul, Shanghai, Tokyo, Vienna, and Warsaw. All suffered major suspensions in activity due to nationalization or war. We know that many investments were completely wiped out, and the average returns for emerging markets would certainly be much lower if these losses were included. Many attractive-looking submerged securities have no value now, except perhaps as collector's items or exotic wallpaper.

And let us not forget that political instability remains with us. Just ask those who purchased stock in the securities markets that existed in Teheran before the Iranian revolution and in Havana before Castro's ascension to power.

The Mexican Roller Coaster

Even without a change of government control, however, political instability can still wreak havoc on the stock markets of emerging countries. The roller-coaster ride in the Mexican market during the mid-1990s, shown in Figure 3-1, aptly illustrates this point.

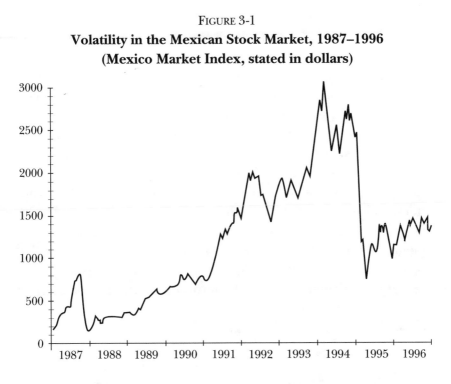

FIGURE 3-1

**Volatility in the Mexican Stock Market, 1987–1996
(Mexico Market Index, stated in dollars)**

SOURCE: Datastream.

During the early 1990s, Mexico was the apple of Wall Street's eye. Under the strong political leadership of a Harvard-educated president, the country was committed to free-market reform. It privatized many state-owned companies and moved decisively to open its markets by signing the North American Free Trade Agreement (NAFTA). It also loosely pegged its currency to the dollar, which made the peso appear to be free of substantial currency risk. As a result, the country was viewed by global investors as the safest emerging market, and billions of investment dollars poured in.

It appears, however, that at Harvard the president had concentrated on politics, rather than economics. With a major presidential election looming in 1994, the governing party wooed the electorate by allowing it to live beyond its means through short-term borrowing abroad. This shaky financial underpinning was blasted almost overnight by the political uncertainties rising from the assassination of a leading presidential candidate and a wide-spread uprising in the southern part of the country. Alarmed by such violent political developments, the short-term capital inflows suddenly evaporated. With little to finance the large trade deficit, the peso collapsed and Mexico was forced to let it float freely against the U.S. dollar. Interest rates soared along with inflation-ary pressures, and eventually austerity policies introduced to re-strain the inflation caused a sharp recession. As the economy fell, so did Mexican stock prices. U.S. investors who sold Mexican stocks during early 1995 faced the worst of all financial worlds: not only was the peso price of the stocks much lower, but the pesos themselves converted into fewer dollars because of their sharp de-preciation. At its nadir, the Mexican stock market lost about 70 percent of its value in U.S. dollar terms from 1994 to 1995.

KEN ALEXANDER
San Francisco Examiner
© *Copley News Service*

A Tale of Two Flies

Political risk is everywhere and cares not where it leaves its tainted trail. It affects the fortunes not only of countries but also of individual companies. In this particular tale, it elevated two little flies to front-page headlines.

India, the second most populous nation with 920 million people, is certainly one of the largest potential markets for Colonel Sanders' Kentucky Fried Chicken (KFC) restaurants. But the battle to establish a beachhead in New Delhi, the capital of India, turned out to be quite a bloody one. Under the slogan "What India needs is computer chips, not potato chips," the nationalist city government was determined to drive Colonel Sanders' troops out of India, the land of tandoori chicken. Finding two flies in the part of the kitchen used to cut up frozen chicken, the city health commissioner immediately canceled KFC's license and shut down the restaurant because of "unsanitary conditions."

Did restaurants owned by Indian nationals have fewer flies? According to many New Delhi residents, the sanitary conditions in the KFC restaurant were superior to those in almost all of the city's 20,000 restaurants, many of which were operating without a license. *The New York Times* quoted M. D. Nalapat, a well-known Indian columnist, as saying that KFC should have been given an award rather than being shut down, "because only two flies were found." Obviously, the issue here was not sanitation but misguided nationalism.

The Mexican crisis and the tale of two flies have taught investors a useful lesson: that politics is still one of the most important sources of risk in emerging markets. Political upheavals can cause serious damage to local economies and investors' confidence. While many emerging markets are moving toward democracy and free markets, thus significantly reducing political risks, many political risks still remain and could have significant impact on returns.

To manage political risk effectively, it is important to know that it is usually made up of two components, country-specific risk and systematic risk. Country-specific risk, such as political scandals and military coups, tends to happen independently in different countries and thus can be reduced by diversification. Systematic political risks, however, tend to affect the returns of developed as well as emerging markets, and they cannot be diversified away. For instance, the stability of China, Russia, and the Middle East has broad implications for world development. As a result, emerging-market securities with significant exposure to these risks should carry extra returns as compensation.

CHAPTER FOUR

Lawlessness Makes Emerging Markets a Dangerous Jungle

HAVE YOU EVER wished for a world without lawyers? Almost five hundred years ago, Thomas More did. In writing his masterpiece *Utopia,* he noted, "They have no lawyers among them, for they consider them as a sort of people whose profession it is to disguise matters." A century later, William Shakespeare took a very direct route to creating a new order: "The first thing we do, let's kill all the lawyers."

Because the whole concept of law is enmeshed in social and cultural development as well as in economic growth, it plays a very different role in developing nations than it does throughout much of Western civilization. While emerging markets have not been able to kill off all the lawyers, they have managed to keep their numbers down by limiting the number of laws. In many developing countries, for example, appropriate contract and other laws simply do not exist. Investors who have fretted over the endless haranguing of lawyers as to appropriate language, covenants, and restrictions suddenly wish for such protective, but expensive, cover when they find themselves facing losses that are unprotected by adequate legal provision.

Even where there are laws, creativity and the right connections allow shrewd entrepreneurs to weave through loopholes. Our favorite example is the story of the Guangzhou Jockey Club in China, as reported in *The Wall Street Journal.*

While gambling is a "capitalist sin" that is officially illegal in China, it is not illegal to hold intelligence contests. With this in mind, officials of the Jockey Club pointed out that horse racing is really a sport in which patrons compete in an intelligence contest; the winners are those who are the most skillful in predicting which Mongolian stallion will finish the race first. And just as sports champions receive prizes, the winners of intelligence contests are entitled to monetary awards. Specious though it may be, this reasoning led to the reestablishment of wagering in China despite the fact that an official ban is still in effect. With a thirty-foot concrete horse standing in front of the main gate of the racetrack, the facility is officially labeled "a brain sports stadium." Not surprisingly, one of the owners of the Guangzhou Jockey Club is none other than the city government.

The Pervasiveness of Lawlessness

For the most part, however, it is lawlessness, rather than creative evasion of laws, that is pervasive throughout emerging markets. In many lands, motorists ignore traffic signals, businessmen rarely pay taxes, policemen moonlight as kidnappers, and nobody trusts the courts. This situation creates an ideal environment for corruption and extortion. Two thousand years ago, the Chinese philosopher Lao-tzu said that "the ideal government is one whose existence you cannot even feel." Businesspeople, however, need good government because even though it may seem invisible, it is still powerful. This is especially true in most emerging markets, where government officials often have unlimited powers but limited accountability. As a result, distortion and extortion can become a way of life for many private businesses. To take just one example, the mistress of a Vietnamese tax official made an unsuccessful foray into the cosmetics industry. Unable to sell her products on the market, she unloaded the lipsticks and creams onto the companies whose tax returns her lover audited. Fearful of an unfavorable review, most of the companies bought her products. She made a handsome profit, and the tax returns were approved.

Government officials are not alone in harassing global bargain hunters. Joint-venture partners and the managers of overseas companies often view investors from developed countries as cash cows to be milked. Many newly privatized firms simply do not care about their shareholders' welfare. In such situations, outside investors often become victims of sweetheart deals between company management and the managers' relatives or corrupt government officials. It is not unusual to have company assets sold to managers' relatives, or to other firms controlled by management, at discount prices. Although such a sale is tantamount to stealing from shareholders, it is extremely costly and difficult for shareholders to take any legal action to protect their interests. "Under communism it used to be a sport to steal from the state," said Professor Rudolf Andorka of Budapest University about the practices of some managers in formerly Communist countries. Now, even though the companies belong to shareholders, the managers' hands are still sticky.

Shareholder activists should be aware that it may not be easy to throw out incompetent and crooked managers. While most managers in emerging markets do not have access to antitakeover lawyers, they have plenty of poison pills for investors to swallow. In Russia, for example, "hostile" shareholders may find that their names have mysteriously disappeared from the company's stockholder record book, wiping out both their investment and their right to vote.

And while nature abhors a vacuum, enterprising criminals thrive in areas where law enforcement is lax or nonexistent. Thus, organized crime has rushed in to control many business operations in the underground economies in Colombia, Mexico, the Philippines, Russia, Taiwan, Thailand, and other emerging markets. Global investors often find themselves unknowingly doing business with gangsters. This is true even for some emerged markets, such as Japan. For example, *The New York Times* reported that the seven largest Japanese real estate lenders had bad loans totaling $77 billion in 1996. As many as 70 percent of these related to the Yakuza, an organization of Japanese gangsters. During the Japanese real estate bubble in the 1980s, the Yakuza had borrowed billions of dollars and then defaulted on the loans when the market crashed.

Some bankers attempted to collect the interest payments or foreclose on the properties, but they quickly found such strategies to be quite dangerous. Two bankers were shot to death, and many others were the targets of death threats and Molotov cocktails. Wisely, perhaps, some banks chose not to try to collect their money. Some delinquent real estate owners even hired Yakuza members to stay in their buildings to prevent banks from foreclosing on the properties.

For the most part, guns are not a major threat to those traveling throughout the world in search of investment riches. Bribery and its handmaiden, corruption, are. Although no strangers to business in developed countries, these two activities are often endemic to commerce in emerging markets. It can, and sometimes is, argued that bribery is a naturally accepted cultural component of many societies. Traditional Chinese religion offers a case in point.

The Kitchen God, acting as the representative of all the gods in Heaven, was said to arrive in every family's kitchen on the first day of the lunar New Year. He kept an eye on the family throughout the year and then left at year's end to report to Heaven on their behavior. A family that got a good report would be rewarded with propitious fortune the following year; one that did not would be punished with bad luck. Eager to get a good report card on the evening of the Kitchen God's departure, many Chinese families believed that they could bribe him with a ritual dinner of sweet dishes and fruits and prayers that he would say "sweet things about them" in Heaven. Not surprisingly, those families who were particularly sinful during the year would offer the most lavish dinners.

In Russia, a venture capitalist named Kharshan received good fortune from the Kitchen God by buying not only dinner but also the Moscow hotel that served the meal. The hotel, The Cosmos, was, and remains to this day, a foreign exchange spigot. With 1,800 rooms, it is Russia's largest hotel for foreign tourists and generates $10 million in profits per year. In the United States, such earnings would easily put the hotel's value at more than $100 million.

Paul Klebnikov, a reporter for *Forbes* magazine, described how "the right connections and a strong dose of guile" had helped Kharshan get the deal of the century:

> As an insider, he knew the hotel, owned by the Russian government and the city of Moscow, was up for privatization. Because of the foreign currency it handles, it was likely to attract a lot of business. Kharshan's first step was to scare away rival bidders. He bribed journalists from two influential business papers to publish negative financial information about the hotel. . . . He also spoke on TV about the poor state of the Russian hotel industry. He bribed government officials to limit the privatization auction to two locations in Moscow instead of many locations around the country. And just in case, Kharshan bribed the managers of two other investment funds not to participate in the auction.

These strategies paid off handsomely. Kharshan was the only serious bidder who showed up. He bought a quarter interest in the Cosmos for $2.5 million, paying essentially 10 cents on the dollar. Nothing in Russian business law prevented such a distortion of a free-market bidding process.

Con Artists Flourish in a World Without Legal Safeguards

Without legal safeguards and requirements for full and honest disclosure of all material information about prospective investments, swindlers and con artists have almost free rein. Two examples should alert investors to the dangers that lurk in the investment hinterlands. Although these frauds caused severe losses for credulous investors, they were lethal only to those who believed that there is a sure path to overnight riches.

MMM Meant Triple Misery for Russian Investors

Russian history and literature abounds with stories of enormous frauds. Nikolai Gogol, in *The Inspector General*, has a whole town believing a character is someone he is not. Russians seem particularly susceptible to advertisements that promise to make them rich. The early 1990s were filled with such advertisements. Many of them appeared shortly after the mass distribution of vouchers that gave citizens the right to purchase securities of newly privatized Russian companies at rock-bottom prices. Swindlers, abetted by a widespread breakdown of law and order, saw a great opportunity and seized it.

Enter Sergei Mavrodi. He saw that runaway inflation was wiping out the modest savings of many humble citizens. Capitalizing on their panic and greed, Mavrodi created the "venture capital" fund MMM. In less than four years, MMM developed into a financial conglomerate—a bank, a voucher investment fund, and an investment company. In February 1994, on national television, Mavrodi introduced an investment program that promised an annual dividend of 3,000 percent. While many were initially suspicious of such an extravagant claim, Mavrodi soothed their fears and fanned their greed by quoting prices of MMM shares twice a week on TV and by providing shareholders the liquidity to receive their capital gains on Thursday for their Tuesday investment.

At first, the shares performed beautifully. They rose from the ruble equivalent of $2 to $10 in less than two months, prompting others to put more money into the fund. Capitalizing on its initial success, Mavrodi launched a TV marketing blizzard, spending 330 million rubles on advertising in March 1994. The MMM commercial, which featured two well-dressed, middle-aged men drinking beer in luxurious Western hotels and promised 3,000 percent annual dividends, was an instant hit. Attracted by promises of apartments in Paris and vacations in San Francisco, 5 million people signed up for shares, turning everyone from poor grandmothers to sturdy generals into shareholding capitalists.

It turned out that the aggressively advertised fund was nothing more than a Ponzi scheme in which early investors were paid fat profits from the investments of those who followed. The technique had been perfected in Boston, Massachusetts, during the 1920s. Charles Ponzi had convinced thousands of investors to hand over $20 million to his "Securities Exchange Company" with a promise of a "50 percent return in forty-five days." Ostensibly, he was to invest in coupons to receive postal stamps that could be redeemed in the United States for more than their cost abroad because European pricing had failed to reflect recent currency devaluations. In fact, only a few hundred dollars of these stamp coupons were available. What Ponzi actually did was to pay off early-bird Peters with the funds received later from gullible Pauls. At first only a handful of investors were willing to throw a hundred-dollar bill onto the flames of their greed. But after the news spread that these early investors had indeed received $150 back in forty-five days, a fire began to rage. Money poured in so quickly that Ponzi hired young women to serve coffee and cake while investors waited in long lines to subscribe. Ponzi skimmed off millions for himself, buying a million-dollar, twenty-acre estate with a staff of fifteen, including armed guards with orders to shoot prowlers on sight, limousines, and even a controlling interest in a Boston bank.

The end began when a young investigative reporter, Clarence Barron (who later founded *Barron's*), exposed the fraud in an analysis in the *Boston Post*. Eventually, the bubble burst. Investors were unable to redeem their promissory notes, and Ponzi was sent to jail and later deported. He died a pauper in the charity ward of a Rio de Janeiro hospital. The concept behind Ponzi's scheme, however, has flourished. You will find variations throughout the world. Indeed, one can say that it has become a classic American export: the Coca-Cola of white-collar crime.

The Mavrodi MMM episode in Russia followed a classic Ponzi story line. Of course, the process of MMM paying huge dividends could continue only if a steadily increasing number of credulous investors provided new money. The soaring prices of the company were fueled not by growing earnings but by people buying shares.

As was the case with Ponzi, MMM did not invest the capital raised from new investors because there were no investments that could generate the kind of returns it promised. The company simply refused to reveal how it made money. According to an MMM spokesperson, such information represented "commercial secrets" that needed to be guarded closely against competitors. But MMM's shareholders did not worry about the lack of information about the company's activities. They wanted to believe in the company, and all they cared about was getting rich quickly.

As the fund continued its spectacular rise, the Russian government became alarmed. President Boris Yeltsin and Prime Minister Viktor Chernomyrdin went on TV in June to caution investors not to invest in MMM. Believing that this was just another example of the government's habit of deceiving its people, Russians kept buying the shares. After being lied to for more than half a century, why should they listen to the government this time? Besides, the two men appearing in the TV commercial were drinking beer. Didn't they look more trustworthy than the vodka-loving, sickly president?

The stock hit its peak of 105,000 rubles (about $50) on July 20, 1994. Trying to warn investors, especially pensioners, about the extremely speculative nature of the company, the Finance Ministry, on July 27, issued a warning about the questionable stock and said that it would not back up any investments in the company. Finally investors began to believe what the government was telling them, and a panic ensued. Four days after the ministry's announcement, the price of the shares had dropped to 1,000 rubles (about 45 cents). Fearing MMM's collapse, about three thousand shareholders gathered outside the company's Moscow office, trying to redeem their shares. Mavrodi claimed that he could not redeem the shares because the central government had ruined him. Russia's most popular stock, owned by 5 million people, became essentially worthless. More than a thousand pensioners and war veterans unsuccessfully petitioned the government for emergency relief. All of them were financially ruined, including Venesky, a World War II hero who lost his life savings, and the widow

Urusova, who, suffering from terminal cancer, had simply sought to accumulate enough money for a proper burial.

In an attempt to punish Mavrodi for setting up the pyramid scheme, the government arrested him on charges of tax evasion. But the ingenious Mavrodi took advantage of a provision in Russia's new constitution that protected the freedom of speech of legislators by exempting them from serving jail sentences. He appealed to his shareholders to vote for him in the upcoming election so that he could recover their investment in MMM. He claimed that it was the state that had crushed MMM and that, if elected, he would fight to give money back to the shareholders. On October 30, 1994, Mavrodi won the election, which enabled him to get out of jail and launch his own political party (appropriately named the Party of People's Capital). He even tried to run for the Russian presidency in 1996. However, MMM investors never saw another ruble.

MMM's collapse serves as a useful lesson for emerging-market investors around the world. If something seems too good to be true, it undoubtedly is. In this case, the Russian government did little to protect individual investors from MMM's fraud. There were few regulations that required companies seeking capital to fully disclose information to investors. Moreover, there were no enforcement actions that the government could take if a company failed to conform to the regulations. There was also no law prohibiting financial fraud. As a result, the MMM scheme caused huge damage to the formation of Russia's capital market and played a big role in setting back the public's confidence in capitalism.

A similar scheme took place in Romania in the summer of 1993, when investors from all over the country lined up to place funds in an investment that promised a 250,000 percent annual rate of interest. They completely ignored the fact that the scheme was running on such a huge scale that, if the promised payments were actually made, the cash outflow would exceed Romania's total output of goods and services in less than six months. Unfortunately for the eager participants, greed often triumphs over rationality.

Harshad Mehta: The Invisible Hand in the Indian Stock Market

Because emerging markets are so volatile, with fortunes made and lost overnight, investors often develop an almost religious belief in market gurus who purport to be able to divine future price changes. In the early 1990s, such a guru appeared in India. His name was Harshad Mehta. The 1992 Indian stock market scandal associated with Mehta showed how a lack of market regulation combined with greed can make investors victims of market manipulation.

According to Suman Dubey of *The Asian Wall Street Journal*, Mehta was born into a rather humble cloth merchant family. Unlike many influential stock market analysts in India who had degrees from prestigious Western universities, Mehta had no degree at all. As the oldest of four children, he tried to get a bachelor's degree in commerce but failed to earn the 40 percent grade required to pass the exams. Living in a working-class neighborhood, he began his stock market apprenticeship in 1980 for a meager $70 monthly salary. Mehta made some large stock bets with other people's money but was wiped out twice in stock market crashes in 1982 and 1986.

Mehta was not easily discouraged, however. He had a marketing genius and an uncanny ability to convince credulous investors that if they handed over their money to him, riches were sure to follow. Mehta's forte was the ability to sell dreams. He explained his past failures as valuable experience for understanding the market. He told prospective investors, "I've gone through speculation. . . . I have the opportunity to be on the floor, knowing the psychology of the investors, . . . the psychology of the institutions, and the psychology of the corporations." Believing that notoriety is the way to attract public attention, he even bought a half-page advertisement in India's widely circulated *Economic Times,* calling himself "a liar" in bold letters and then promoting the investment strategies of his perfectly named Growmore Research and Asset Management Company. He demonstrated his financial success, which came from skimming large management fees from his company, by owning a fleet of twenty-nine luxury cars. He favored his chauffeur-driven Lexus and loved to be photographed by news reporters in front of it. In his heyday, Mehta claimed that he was the largest taxpayer in India and boasted that he would pay the government 2.65 billion rupees ($89 million) in taxes for the fiscal year ending in March 1992.

Mehta's company was not a Ponzi front. With a great deal of luck and undeniable daring, he started off with some notable successes. He bought shares of Associated Cement Company at 350 rupees a share and watched the stock price increase to more than 10,500 rupees in eighteen months. Because of his marketing savvy and his brief but strong track record in the early 1990s, Mehta soon became one of the most powerful gurus in the Bombay market. *The Asian Wall Street Journal* quoted a broker who said that Mr. Mehta "acquired a large following of brokers, and whatever he touched was picked up by them. If Harshad bought 1,000 shares of a company, the others bought up 10,000." With such a large group of disciples, his purchase (or rumor of purchase) could often lead to a self-fulfilling buying spree that sent share prices soaring.

None of Mehta's schemes was as grand as his acquisition of the Mazda Industry and Leasing Ltd. of India (not related to the Japanese Mazda Motor Company). At the time of the purchase, the company had run up a huge liability of 1.3 billion rupees, and the shares were trading at around 8 rupees. Mehta bought a controlling stake of 33 percent in August 1991. Through a combination of financial restructuring, diversification into real estate and other investments, and rather creative accounting, he parlayed Mazda's substantial losses into a 650-million-rupee profit for the six months ending in March 1992. When the news of his acquisition hit the market in September 1991, speculators ranging from "Bombay lift attendants to Gujarati peasants" surged to buy, and their frenzy created one of the largest bubbles in the history of investment, larger than the British South Sea Bubble. Mazda's price soared from 8 rupees to 1,600 rupees in seven months (see Figure 4-1), gaining more than 200 times its original value and hitting a staggering P/E ratio of 1,189 on March 31, 1992, based on dubious earnings at best.

Was 1,189 times earnings too much to pay for any company, especially one whose financial history was one of large losses? Not when the company was managed by the legendary Mehta, who

FIGURE 4-1

Prices of Common Stock of Mazda Industry and Leasing Ltd., July 1991 through Suspension of Trading, June 10, 1992

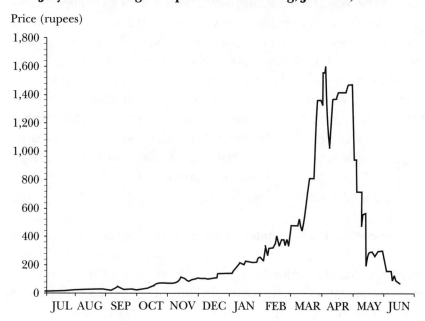

Price (rupees)

SOURCE: Datastream.

had turned himself from a financially broken man into the country's largest taxpayer in less than four years. Thus, when Mehta's investors found out that he was going to diversify Mazda's operation into more lucrative real estate and money management, they simply could not contain their excitement. Imagine what would happen to the company's earnings if Mehta picked a few more investments like Associated Cement! The optimism over Mazda's prospects also spread to other stocks. The Bombay Stock Exchange Index (Sensex) rose from 1,950 to 3,000 and passed the 4,300 level in less than three months. Mehta earned himself the nickname the "Big Bull of the Bombay stock market," and *The Asian Wall Street Journal* called him "a symbol of the stock market boom" in India. In Bombay, teenagers began wearing T-shirts with the inscription "I Love Harshad."

The meteoric rise of Mazda came to a sudden halt when the Reserve Bank of India, the country's central bank, discovered in late April 1992 that billions of rupees were missing from many of India's prestigious banks. Mehta became the focus of government investigation and the prime suspect behind the missing funds. According to a report by Agence France Presse, "Mehta was accused of siphoning money from the government bond market in connivance with obliging banking executives and investing it in the stock market for personal profit." News reports alleged that he had used the diverted funds to buy up the issues in which he had invested, such as Mazda, triggering a spree that had grossly inflated their prices, and that he had then sold the shares at a huge profit, creating panic among other subscribers, who sold at a loss. The Central Bureau of Investigation arrested Mehta "in connection with India's billion dollar stock-market scandal," charging him with "conspiracy, forgery, and cheating." The government also ordered the seizure of his assets and froze his bank accounts.

Battered by the scandal, Mazda's price dropped like a rock, until trading in the stock was finally suspended in June 1992. The once sensational Sensex also lost its appeal, falling more than 30 percent and wiping out $25 billion in share values after the government investigation was announced. Many unfortunate investors found that what "grew more" was their pain rather than their wealth. Several large financial institutions were also badly burned by the scandal, and the head of one of the banks involved with Mehta died of a heart attack after he learned that his bank was missing billions of rupees. Mehta spent some time in jail and will probably be entangled in civil lawsuits for the rest of his life.

Thus ended the biggest financial fraud in the history of India.

The popular joke in financial circles in India went as follows. Question: "Is Harshad Mehta an honest broker?" Answer: "Honest, you can't get any broker."

Other Complications of Emerging-Market Investing

Political instability and lawlessness are not the only drawbacks of investing in emerging markets. Lack of market liquidity and high trading costs are also detriments. In Zimbabwe, for example, the total market capitalization for all stocks available for purchase by foreign investors in 1996 was only $370 million. Since many mutual funds and pension funds in the United States are more than ten times as large (the largest U.S. mutual fund, the Magellan Fund, had more than $50 billion in assets in 1997), it is clear that the Zimbabwe market is far too small to be a viable outlet for U.S. institutional investors. Several other emerging markets in eastern Europe and the Middle East are also much too small to represent a viable outlet for large institutional investors. Moreover, the transactions costs of dealing in the stocks of emerging-market countries are likely to be several times greater than the equivalent costs in developed countries.

Transactions costs come in four primary guises. First, there is a commission that is paid to the broker arranging the trade. Then there may be a variety of "stamp taxes" paid on either the purchase or the sale of the securities or on both sides of the transaction. Third, there is the so-called bid–asked spread. A market maker may quote the price of IBM common stock as $80 bid, $80¼ asked. This means that if you want to buy IBM stock, the asking price is $80.25. On the other hand, if you wish to sell IBM shares, you will receive only $80. The $0.25 difference is the middleman's markup, or spread. If an investor buys IBM and then sells it later, she will have to pay two commissions, one for buying and one for selling, as well as the total bid–asked spread. Table 4-1 shows the total of the first three transactions costs for some selected emerging markets as well as for three developed countries.

Note that the cost of these three items alone is almost nine times as high in Korea as in the United States. And we have not used the highest transactions costs illustrations. Barings Securities has estimated that the bid–asked spread in the Chilean market is almost 4 percent, and Morgan Stanley estimates that the spread in the Indian market is as high as 3 percent.

TABLE 4-1

Illustrative Transactions Costs for Investors, Purchase and Later Sale of an Individual Stock

Country	Commission (%)	Stamp Taxes (%)	Bid–Asked Spread (%)	Total
Argentina	1.00	0.48	1.25	2.73
Brazil	1.00	0.14	2.48	3.62
Indonesia	1.30	0.30	1.50	3.10
Korea	0.80	0.50	2.25	3.55
Malaysia	1.20	0.10	1.09	2.39
Thailand	1.30	—	1.89	3.19
Germany	0.50	—	0.49	0.99
Japan	0.40	0.30	0.75	1.45
United States	0.13	—	0.27	0.40

SOURCE: Morgan Stanley International Portfolio Desk; authors' estimates.

There is a fourth transactions cost that is harder to measure but is undoubtedly significantly higher in emerging markets than in the far more liquid and actively traded developed markets. Suppose approximately 1,000 shares of XYZ company are traded daily, and the stock is quoted at 49½ bid–50 asked. Now let's imagine that an institutional investor wants to get hold of 10,000 shares of the stock and starts a process of actively bidding for the shares. The problem is that the quote on the shares is unlikely to stay at 49½–50. If the investor buys 1,000 shares the first day at 50, it is quite likely that the stock may be quoted 49¾–50¼, or even 50–50½ the next day. The very process of purchasing a block of stock is likely to drive up its price, just as the sale of a block will tend to depress share prices. In less liquid emerging markets, this effect will tend to be greater than in developed markets, further increasing the cost of trading.

Another trading hazard related to poor liquidity and high transactions costs is the presence of settlement risk. Many emerging markets have antiquated trading systems that are ill equipped for settling large trades. For instance, because there is no computer settlement system in India, brokers must literally move mountains of paper in order to settle a $50 million trade. It could take several weeks to gather up the certificates, since they are often in small denominations of less than one hundred shares each. Then every certificate has to be physically signed by both buyer and seller, a daunting task that may take many months to accomplish. As a result, it might take up to a year to get delivery of the securities for a large trade. In the meantime, market conditions could change and investors would find it difficult to sell their stocks without physical possession of the securities. In Part III, we will discuss certain techniques that can help investors reduce settlement risks and transactions costs.

CHAPTER FIVE

Volatility Guarantees a Bumpy Investment Ride

IF THERE IS one general statement describing the entire emerging-market investment scene, it is that it is a volatile one. This road to riches is not for the fainthearted. You are always guaranteed greater roller-coaster financial results abroad than at home. In 1993, as just one example, an index of securities in the newly established Polish stock market rose almost tenfold during the year. Think of it: a $10,000 investment worth almost $100,000 while investors just sat back and watched it grow! But suppose that a friend of yours was getting so rich and that you wanted a piece of the action, too. So you bought in at $100,000 at the start of 1994. Had you done so, you would have lost more than $50,000 in the first few months of the year. That is the kind of volatility you will face as you invest in the emerging-markets frontier.

Speculation concerning future short-term price movements always plays a role in the ups and downs of markets. The price of any asset is at least partly dependent on future events and thus is subject to spurious or enthusiastic crystal-ball gazing. And since readily marketable assets, such as common stocks, depend on what investors think others might be willing to pay, such gazing is often furthered by wishful thinking. This last phenomenon is sometimes called "The Greater Fool Theory." While you are smart enough to accurately estimate the worth of a stock at 20, you might be willing to pay 30 for it if you believed some greater fool would later buy it at 40. The problem is that there is not an inexhaustible supply of greater fools.

The Dutch were among the first to experience this truth. In seventeenth-century Holland, they engaged in a speculative mania in which tulip bulb prices doubled in a matter of days, then doubled again in the next few days. The scope of the increase is hard to imagine. At the height of the Dutch affair, the price of a single rare bulb rose to a value equivalent to a Mercedes-Benz automobile today. Although most rational Dutch did not believe a tulip bulb could really be "worth" that much, they did believe that some credulous buyer would come along and purchase the bulb at an even higher price.

They not only paid dearly for such fallacious thinking but were responsible for an investing term known as "tulipmania," which describes a situation in which reason abdicates to greed and enthrones volatility. Such manias in stock markets were repeated in nineteenth-century England during the South Sea Bubble, in the United States during the late 1920s, and in Japan during the late 1980s. In each instance, the bubble burst and many speculators were financially ruined. With widespread political instability and a lack of rules and regulations, emerging markets routinely experience this situation. It is a risk that investors in these markets must always keep in mind. The following two examples clearly illustrate why.

Taiwan Takes Its Ups and Downs

In the late 1980s, conditions were ripe for a major bull market in Taiwan. The economy was enjoying unprecedented prosperity. Relations with mainland China had warmed after years of social, political, and economic reforms. Many Taiwanese believed that their economy would grow from a small tiger into a giant one, rivaling Japan in economic prosperity. This euphoria, together with huge household savings, led investors on a buying spree. It started in 1987, when the Taiwan Stock Market Index rose 125 percent. In 1988, the market soared again, by 118 percent; in 1989, it jumped another 88 percent (see Figure 5-1). During this powerful three-year bull market, the average P/E ratio skyrocketed from the mid-20s to an eye-popping 95 times earnings. Some market watchers advised caution, but most investors were not alarmed. If buyers today would pay 95 times earnings for stocks, why wouldn't they pay 100 times tomorrow?

FIGURE 5-1

Taiwan Stock Market Index

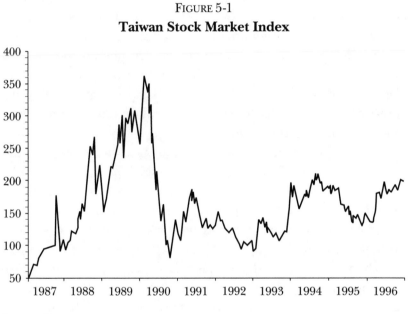

SOURCE: Datastream.

For a while, it seemed everybody was in the market and making money. Trading became a national pastime, often driven by rumors of what the "smart money" was doing. The big traders, or insiders, who could move markets were known as the "big hands." A stock would be touted simply because "Lin the Wealthy" or "Big Player Lee" was buying. Housewives formed investment clubs over tea and became aggressive traders, changing positions several times a day. Under peer pressure, some of these normally conservative women would put the family nest egg on the line as they rolled their investment dice. Frantic trading by all caused shares to turn over an average of more than seven times per year. (For comparison, shares in the United States turn over an average of once every 25 months.)

While Taiwan did have margin requirements (limiting the amount that could legally be borrowed to finance stock market speculation), they did not deter speculators from using illegal lenders, such as loan sharks, to finance their stock market purchases. Even though these loan sharks charged interest that compounded at rates as high as 20 percent per month (which meant that a stock price had to go up almost 800 percent per year to break even), there were still large numbers of speculators who liked the odds. It was reported that illegal margin trading accounted for as much as 40 percent of total trading on the Taiwan Stock Exchange at the time.

The nationwide speculative mania took unexpected tolls on the island's quality of life and economy. It was difficult, for example, to get a taxi during trading hours because most drivers were busy following the market and "placing bets" with their brokers. Many construction sites were deserted by workers who found it more profitable to mix stocks rather than concrete. Projects slipped years behind schedule. There was even a proposal by the government to move trading hours from 9:00 A.M.–12:00 noon to 12:00–3:00 P.M. so that workers could use their lunch breaks to execute trades and be less disruptive to regular business. Some commentators suggested that R.O.C. really stood for "Republic of Casino" rather than the island's official name, The Republic of China. The quick-money mentality became so damaging and disruptive to Taiwanese culture and development that social conservatives began to pray for a market crash to restore traditional values.

Their prayers were answered. Prompted by the government's decision to impose a transaction tax to curb the rampant speculation and increased uncertainty engendered by the Persian Gulf War, the "big hands" decided to cash in their chips. The Taiwan

Stock Market Index dropped almost 80 percent in less than nine months, wiping out $184 billion of investor wealth. This translates to a staggering loss of $9,200 per person for its 20 million residents! Hundreds of thousands of investors were financially ruined, especially those margin investors who had borrowed money from gang-related loan sharks. As shown in Figure 5-1, the Taiwanese market had yet to digest its excesses even six years after the crash.

BY MORRIS DOCKTOR & XU JUNG

"Wah!!!"

There is one lesson that cries out when "tulipmania" strikes any market, including those in developed nations: investors should always look at the valuation standards that generally characterize stock markets. It is not difficult to spot when these are completely out of whack with historic levels. The crude P/E ratio is certainly one such standard. The Taiwanese stocks, for example, generally sold at a P/E ratio of 16 to 22. Some may reasonably argue that slightly higher ratios might be acceptable at certain times, such as at a cyclical low (when earnings tend to be depressed) or in a very-low-interest-rate environment. During the boom times of 1989, however, Taiwanese stocks sold at more than 90 times earnings. There was no way such a multiple could be justified. Similarly, Taiwanese stocks sold at multiples of book value that were unprecedented, not only in Taiwan's history but also by the standards of world markets. At the very least, investors should have pared back their holdings of Taiwanese stocks so they would not get out of line with the relative size of the country as a whole.

Happy Flying Crashes in China

At the start of the 1990s, the People's Republic of China underwent a remarkable change. Under Deng Xiaoping's market-reform policy, many state enterprises were partially privatized and stocks representing ownership interest were issued to the public. For most Chinese, these stocks represented a once-in-a-lifetime opportunity, both literally and figuratively. After all, many of the now partially public companies enjoyed near-monopoly situations, and China's 1.2 billion people constituted the largest potential market in the world. Never before in most of those people's lifetimes had they been given the chance to buy the first issue of the next Microsoft. Who would want to acknowledge that while many Chinese companies had strong growth potential, it was less clear how their managers would turn this potential into earnings growth? And who would want to admit that how these companies would survive foreign competition was an even murkier question? These little shadows were ignored. So, too, was the fact that political uncertainty is always associated with the transition from a controlled to a market economy and, as such, deserves a proper risk premium in the form of extra returns. In the boom period of 1991–1993, "plunging into sea" (private business) was the magic phrase in the People's Republic of China. With unbounded enthusiasm, its citizens created a spectacular stock market boom and bust.

While getting in on the ground floor was an act of wisdom, later purchase behavior quickly became insane. Beginning in 1992, the Shanghai Stock Exchange Index went from 100 to 200 in less than four months and then quickly doubled again during the feverish trading days of late May. By mid-1992, the conventional rule that stocks should sell at a multiple of 10 to 30 times their earnings was completely abandoned. Multiples of 50 to 100 times earnings became the norm on the Shanghai stock Exchange. Some "hot" issues fetched even higher multiples. At one point, Happy Flying (Feile), a consumer electronics company, sold for more than 1,000 times its previous year's earnings. That was happy flying indeed.

Such high multiples should always prompt skepticism. During the heyday of the 1992 boom, any such skepticism was viewed as heresy. Most investors firmly believed that the Chinese economy would take off and that the earnings of Happy Flying would rise like a rocket as a result of equipping 1.2 billion consumers with TVs and VCRs. This vision justified their belief that although the earnings multiple of the stock would undoubtedly shrink, investors all over the world would eagerly pay even higher prices for the shares.

Many academics and researchers watched the Shanghai stock market in awe. A respected Chinese finance professor tells the story of a conversation he had with a college freshman. Having made a good deal of money in Happy Flying, the eighteen-year-old pronounced it would "fly even higher" and proposed to buy still more shares at a P/E ratio of 600. The professor advised caution. To his embarrassment, the student turned out—at least for a while—to be right.

The government's control over initial public offerings (IPOs) also helped drive share prices higher. With IPO prices set below market-clearing levels, these new issues became so hot that investors literally had to line up overnight to purchase them. According to a recent study, the average IPO profit was 150 percent on the first trading day, further creating the impression that there was easy money to be made in the stock market. This IPO underpricing was probably the largest in the world history of new issues, and it caused many fraudulent and corrupt practices in the market.

For example, some investment bankers would keep a large block of securities off the market when the IPO started trading. This would make the supply so tight that the price would rise quickly in the aftermarket. In one "hot" issue whose price quadrupled on the first day of trading, a considerable portion of the offering was sold to corporate managers, government officials, relatives of managers and officials, and other people with connections. These buyers were advised to hold on to their allotments until the shares could be sold later at much higher prices.

The tight government control of the Chinese stock market also gave investors a false sense of security. *The Wall Street Journal* quoted a Shanghai investor as saying that "the government won't let bad companies on the market, and the government doesn't want prices to fall—so a socialist market can only go up." Even top government officials thought the market could not crash. A senior market regulator was quoted as saying, "With socialism, we have the tools to prevent the stock market from booming or crashing."

With apparently unlimited upside potential and virtually no downside risk, investors all over China launched an IPO buying spree. In August 1992, when news of an impending IPO in Shenzhen was revealed, 3 million frenzied investors crowded into the city carrying bags and suitcases full of cash. They arrived by air, sea, and land, quickly filling every hotel room in the city of 2 million people. Many eager investors had to sleep in the streets. As it turned out, the issue was so tightly rationed that few investors were actually able to buy shares. Outraged, those who had been unsuccessful in purchasing stock rioted in the streets to protest the uneven distribution of IPO shares.

Then Happy Flying fell. Perhaps the student finally decided to follow his professor's advice. Who knows? In any case, as some investors decided to cash in their profits, the stock began to fall. The sudden realization that prices could go down triggered a selling blizzard, causing the entire Shanghai stock market to drop 75 percent in five months, as is shown in Figure 5.2. Happy Flying not only led the way but also, with the hot air gone, crashed more spectacularly than any other stock, dropping from 14.77 to 2.60 yuan. When it hit bottom in November, it was just about at its new-issue price.

FIGURE 5-2

Price Index for the Shanghai Stock Market Class A Share Index, January 1992–December 1995 (January 1, 1992 = 100)

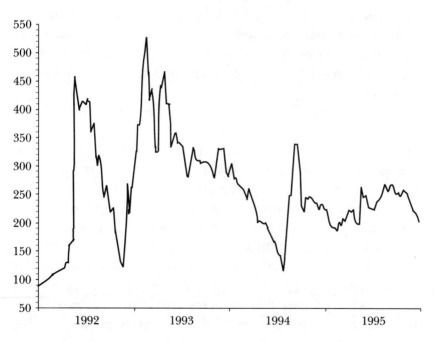

SOURCE: Datastream.

The most remarkable thing about the Shanghai market, however, was the extremely short memory of its investors. Within a few
days of hitting bottom, speculation pushed the market back up.
This time, the tempo was even more torrid. Driven by rumors of a
government rescue, those who had lost a fortune in the June crash
quickly rebuilt their positions by borrowing money from friends
and relatives. In just three months, the overall market index flew
from a low of 120 up to a new height of 538. Once again, profit
taking started and the market slid precipitously. Many investors
lost their own money in the first bubble and then their friends'
and relatives' money in the second.

The General Evidence on Emerging-Market Volatility

While the previous examples are extreme, they are nevertheless
part of an overall pattern: emerging markets are, by their nature,
extremely volatile compared with developed markets. This is a fact
that investors must always keep in mind. An exhaustive study that
we conducted proves this point. We used data covering the twenty-
year period from 1976 to 1995 and came up with the results in
Table 5-1.

Obviously, several emerging stock markets have provided generous total rates of return over the twenty-year period. Many
of these returns, including dividends and capital gains, have exceeded the returns on U.S. stocks by a substantial margin. And
just as obviously, not every emerging market has done as well as
the U.S. market. The data also show that emerging-market stock
returns are highly variable, as indicated by the range of annual returns and the index of the variance of stock prices shown in adja-
cent columns of the table. Returns on Argentine equities, for
example, have ranged from a gain of more than 450 percent in
1976 to a loss of more than 62 percent in 1990. That market has
been more than ten times as volatile as the U.S. market over the
twenty-year period. Clearly, the extra returns that have been avail-

able to investors from emerging markets have come at the expense of assuming considerably higher volatility. Moreover, accepting more volatility has not been a guarantee of extraordinarily high returns, as is shown in the cases of Brazil and Greece.

TABLE 5-1

Average Dollar Return and Volatility of Selected Markets, 1976–1995

Country	Average Annual Return (%)	Number of Years in which Returns Were Positive	Number of Years in which Returns Were Negative	Highest Yearly Return (%)	Lowest Yearly Return (%)	Volatility Index (United States=100)
Argentina	23.7	11	9	456.5	−61.9	1,073
Brazil	2.7	9	11	158.0	−66.7	440
Chile	27.3	15	5	141.9	−56.9	407
Greece	−0.02	10	10	141.1	−57.3	368
Hong Kong	22.3	15	5	117.1	−42.8	208
India	11.8	14	6	103.3	−34.2	201
Thailand	16.0	12	8	123.1	−36.2	326
United States	14.2	16	4	36.8	−6.6	100

DATA SOURCE: International Finance Corporation.

There have been periods of several years or longer when some emerging markets have consistently produced negative rates of return for investors. For instance, the Chilean equity index dropped from 866 in 1980 to 100 in 1984, losing almost 90 percent of its value over the four years. The two-thirds decline in the Brazilian stock market average during 1990 is the most dramatic change in stock prices in a single year. Moreover, there is no guarantee that the high returns of the past twenty years in markets such as Argentina will persist. On the other hand, the laggards, such as Brazil and Greece, may turn in stellar performances in the future.

What Is a Global Bargain Hunter to Do?

We have seen that life on the investment frontier is truly wild. It is easy to get carried away imagining the huge profits that lie ahead from investing in emerging markets. Dreams of billions of Chinese and Indians diligently working and producing extraordinary rates of growth for their economies can increase the pulse rate of any investor. High volatility is the inevitable result of such dreams.

We have also seen that an investor who purchases securities in emerging markets accepts many special risks. The quality of the accounting information released by companies in emerging markets and the ethical standards of business behavior sometimes leave much to be desired. Accurate information is often very difficult to obtain, and history is full of examples of sovereign governments breaking their promises to investors and expropriating private property. Political risks are substantial, and it is costly and difficult to sell one's holdings in illiquid emerging markets. How can a successful bargain hunt be carried out under such volatile conditions and with such obvious and hidden dangers?

CHAPTER SIX

How Diversification Can Reduce Risk

NOT ONLY DO emerging stock markets provide investors with particularly attractive growth prospects, their stocks can also be purchased at price levels generally well below those in developed markets. That's the good news. The bad news is that emerging markets are extremely risky. Does the bad news cancel out the good? Of course not. There is a way to protect yourself by obtaining a kind of financial travel insurance that gives you a measure of safety and security on your global bargain hunt. It comes in the form of broad diversification, the most time-honored method of risk reduction. As Miguel de Cervantes wrote in *Don Quixote* four hundred years ago, "'Tis the part of a wise man to keep himself today for tomorrow, and not venture all his eggs in one basket."

What writers have known for centuries, economists began to analyze rigorously only four decades ago. One economist, Harry Markowitz, so refined Cervantes's observation that he went on to win a Nobel Prize in Economics in 1990. Markowitz proved that it is both prudent and profitable to allocate your eggs among many baskets. In other words, by including investments in emerging markets in your portfolio, you may actually incur *less* risk than if you had only domestic holdings. Because the subject is so important, let us review the theory of diversification and demonstrate its practical and profitable effects.

Diversification Provides Protection

Since investing abroad, especially in emerging markets, is inherently riskier than socking away money in domestic assets, many investors assume that adding emerging-market securities to a portfolio of U.S. stocks will increase their risk. In fact, a growing body of analytic and historical evidence clearly demonstrates that some degree of global diversification actually *decreases* overall portfolio risk.

Does this mean you will never lose money? Not necessarily. What it does mean is that broad diversification protects you by dampening volatility, which is the degree of instability in returns (or valuation ups and downs) that the investment community considers to be a measure of risk. For example, if one portfolio consistently earns 10 percent each and every year, it is considered much less risky than a second portfolio that returns an *average* 10 percent annual return but whose annual result varies widely from large losses to extraordinary gains. Volatility is a rough but readily useful guide to the riskiness of any portfolio.

The idea of spreading investments around to protect the stability of an investment portfolio is based on the theory of optimal portfolio diversification, a brilliant concept developed by Harry Markowitz in the 1950s. Capitalizing on the ability of the then newly developed computers to crunch huge databases, Markowitz showed how to create securities portfolios that were optimally balanced to minimize risk. It is generally true that riskier securities offer greater rates of return—risk has its rewards. Investors are compensated for being exposed to greater possibilities for loss and disappointment. But it is sometimes possible to combine securities in a portfolio in such a way as to obtain both *higher* returns and *less* risk.

Markowitz showed that in some circumstances the addition of risky holdings in portfolios can produce higher profits as well as greater protection against loss. It sounds like an oxymoronic statement, but actually, it was a profound insight. Today Markowitz's pathbreaking analysis is routinely taught in economics departments and business schools around the world, as well as being used by most professional investment managers to improve portfolio performance. The trick is to find combinations of securities whose returns are not highly correlated. Then, if one market or industry goes into a tailspin, the resulting losses will be counterbalanced by stability, or even positive developments, in other markets. For example, a portfolio consisting of Ford and General Motors is highly, or positively, correlated since all companies in the auto industry tend to rise and fall together. A portfolio of General Motors and Exxon, on the other hand, would have a much lower correlation and would thus provide considerable possibilities for risk reduction. In some periods the correlation might even be negative, since a rise in the price of gasoline, which would result in less travel by car and thus hurt General Motors, would provide Exxon with higher prices at the pump.

Diversification in Theory

A simple example illustrates the potential benefits of diversification. Let us suppose we have two contiguous countries: Sun Country, located at the bottom of a mountain, and Ski Country, on top. Tourism is the main business of both countries. Sun Country is endowed with sparkling beaches, tennis courts, swimming pools, and golf courses. When the weather is dry, its economy booms. Unfortunately, there are many years in which it rains continuously, and the country's resorts suffer badly. Ski Country features majestic mountains and the best alpine skiing in the world. When Mother Nature cooperates with abundant precipitation and heavy snow cover, the resorts of Ski Country are always full and business is brisk.

Now suppose that half the years are sunny and dry and the other half are snowy and wet, and that the fortunes of both economies are entirely dependent on the weather. During sunny years, Sun Country booms and stocks in its industries produce 50 percent rates of return. During seasons with continuous precipitation, however, travelers stay away and investors lose 25 percent of their stakes. If half the seasons are dry and half are wet, Sun Country's investors will earn an average return of 12.5 percent per year. Investors putting up $200 will make $100 in dry seasons, while they lose $50 in wet ones. On average, they will receive $50 every two years, or $25 per year, which is 12.5 percent of their $200 investment.

Now consider the case for investors in Ski Country. The situation is exactly the same, except that the years are reversed. During wet years, Ski Country investors will make 50 percent profits, but when the weather is dry and ski conditions are poor, they will lose 25 percent. Again, on average, investors will earn a 12.5 percent rate of return. If the years alternated predictably between wet and dry, investors who could hold on for two years would come out fine. But, in fact, weather patterns are unpredictable. There is no way of knowing what the weather will be in any given year, and there is a high probability of volatility in either investment. Indeed, there could be several wet seasons in a row, which would drown investors in Sun Country with annual losses of 25 percent. Should there be a prolonged hot and dry period over several years, however, the assets of Ski Country investors would melt down the increasingly bare slopes. Clearly, concentrating one's investments in either country could be disastrous.

Employing a strategy of diversification, however, will eliminate risk and guarantee a steady 12.5 percent return *each and every year.* Rather than putting all $200 into stocks in one country, an investor should put $100 into Sun Country and $100 into Ski Country. When the weather is dry, she will make $50 on her Sun Country investments and lose $25 on her Ski Country investments. The total return is $25 ($50 − $25) on an investment of $200, or 12.5 percent. If, instead, the weather is wet, she will lose $25 on her Sun Country investments but earn $50 from her Ski Country holdings. Again, she will make 12.5 percent. So whatever the weather, year after year she will earn a steady, risk-free 12.5 percent. Even though investment in either country is very volatile and risky, risk is completely eliminated by diversifying across countries.

This is the magic of diversification. No matter what the weather, by diversifying investments over both countries, an investor is sure of making a 12.5 percent return each year. The trick that makes the game work is that while both countries are risky (their returns are highly variable from one year to another), they are affected differently by climate. (In statistical terms, the two countries have a perfect negative correlation.)

Obviously, the benefits of diversification are unlikely to be as complete in practice as in our illustration. It is often the case that world economic conditions affect all countries similarly, at least to some extent. For example, a worldwide recession may affect Sun Country and Ski Country as consumers eschew vacations. Nevertheless, as long as there is at least some lack of parallelism in the fortunes of different companies or countries, diversification will reduce risk. And the lower the correlations between different companies or countries, the more risk reduction can be achieved through diversification.

In practice, even in an integrated world economy, events have different effects on different national economies. The oil crisis of the 1970s, for example, had a more devastating effect on oil-poor Europe and Japan than on the United States, which is at least partially self-sufficient in oil. On the other hand, the tenfold increase in the price of oil had a very positive effect on Indonesia, Venezuela, and oil-producing countries in the Middle East. Similarly, increases in mineral and other raw material prices have positive effects on nations rich in natural resources and negative effects on many developed manufacturing countries.

Correlation coefficients are used to measure the extent to which different markets hit their peaks and valleys at different times. They are the key element in Markowitz's analysis. A perfect positive correlation (a correlation coefficient of +1) indicates that two markets are in lockstep, moving up and down at precisely the same times. A perfect negative correlation (a correlation coefficient of −1) means that two markets always move in opposite directions: whenever one zigs, the other zags. When two markets have a perfect negative correlation—as was the case in our two mythical resort economies—an investor can eliminate risk completely by diversifying.

It is obvious that perfect negative correlation does not exist, although it is certainly a handy concept to illustrate the benefits of diversification. Markowitz's great contribution to investors' wallets was his demonstration that anything less than perfect positive correlation can potentially reduce risk. In other words, perfect negative correlation is not needed to achieve risk reduction from diversification. What is necessary is that economic conditions in different national markets not always be perfectly synchronized. Table 6-1 shows the crucial role of the correlation coefficient in determining the extent to which diversification can reduce risk.

TABLE 6-1
The Correlation Coefficient and Diversification's Ability to Reduce Risk*

Correlation Coefficient	Effect of Diversification on Risk
+1.0	No risk reduction is possible.
0.5	Moderate risk reduction is possible.
0	Considerable risk reduction is possible.
−0.5	Most risk can be eliminated.
−1.0	All risk can be eliminated.

*The less correlated stocks in different markets are, the greater the risk reduction benefits of diversification.

Diversification in Practice

To translate diversification theory into practice, let us first look at the benefits that have been available for an investor in the United States who decides to include foreign stocks in developed markets in his portfolio. We will use two indices on the following pages to represent the investment options available: the Standard & Poor's 500 Stock Index (S&P 500 Index), which represents U.S. common stocks, and the Morgan Stanley Index of European and Far Eastern Stocks (EAFE Index), which represents foreign securities.

Let us now focus on different portfolios' return and risk—or avoidance of risk, which we will call "safety." The standard way of measuring the returns from an individual stock or a portfolio is by calculating total return, based on dividends and changes in the price of the shares. For example, suppose shares of IBM start the year selling at $80 per share. Assume that during the year, IBM pays a $1 dividend and that it sells at $87 at the end of the year. The total return on holding IBM shares during the year is found by adding the $1 dividend and the $7 capital gain resulting from the rise in the price of the stock and dividing the $8 total by the initial price of $80 ($8 ÷ $80 = .10, or 10%). This same technique can be used to measure the returns on a portfolio of securities.

Risk is generally measured as the variability, or variance, of returns from year to year. A portfolio whose return never strayed very far from 10 percent per year, and might return 8 or 9 percent in poor years, would be considered very safe. Its risk or volatility would be low and its safety level high. On the other hand, another portfolio that had an average return of 10 percent but varied substantially from year to year (in bad years it could lose a great deal of money) would be considered very risky and have a low safety rating. The lower the volatility of a portfolio and the greater the stability of its returns from period to period, the safer it is considered to be.

We can construct risk/return graphs—really safety/return graphs—to illustrate the menu of trade-offs between safety and return that have been available to investors in the recent past. These graphs, used throughout this chapter, have the degree of safety on the vertical axis. Since safety is most preferable, the safest (lowest-volatility) rating is at the top, and the least safe (greatest-risk) rating is at the bottom. Annual percentage rates of return are plotted on the horizontal axis and appear from lowest on the left to highest on the right. The goal is to visually present the combination of securities that produces the greatest reward possible with the least amount of risk. Clearly, the objective is to pick a combination that is high in the graph (achieving a desired level of safety) while moving as far as possible to the right (achieving an attractive rate of return).

The Gains from Global Diversification, 1985–1995

During the eleven years ending in the mid-1990s, foreign stocks (in the EAFE Index of developed countries) had an average annual return that was slightly higher than that on U.S. stocks (in the S&P 500 Index). U.S. stocks, however, were safer in that their year-to-year returns were less volatile. The correlation between the returns from the two indexes during this time period was approximately 0.5—positive but only moderately high. Figure 6-1 shows the different combinations of return and safety that could have been achieved if an investor had held different combinations of U.S. and EAFE (developed-country) foreign stocks. At the right-hand side of Figure 6-1, we see the higher return and lower safety level (greater volatility) that would have been achieved with a portfolio of only EAFE stocks. At the left-hand side of the figure, the return on and safety level of a totally domestic portfolio of U.S. stocks are shown. The solid dark line portrays the different combinations of return and safety that would result from different portfolio allocations between domestic and foreign stocks.

Note that as the portfolio shifts from a 100 percent domestic allocation to one with gradual additions of foreign stocks, the return tends to increase because EAFE stocks produced a higher return than domestic stocks over this eleven-year period. The significant point, however, is that adding some of these riskier securities actually increases the portfolio's safety level—at least for a while. Eventually, however, as larger and larger proportions of the riskier EAFE stocks are put into the portfolio, the overall risk rises (the safety level decreases) with the overall return.

FIGURE 6-1

Optimum Stock Mix of U.S. and Developed-Country Stocks

Over an eleven-year period ending in 1995, the mix
that provided the highest return achievable with the least
risk was 30% developed-country stocks and 70% U.S. stocks.

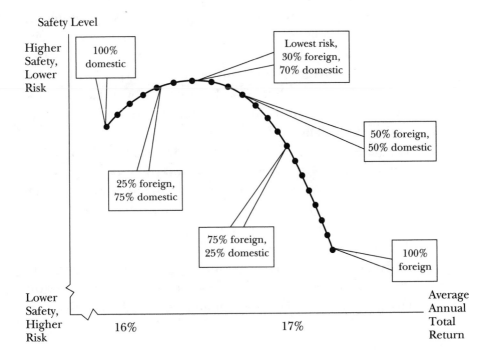

The paradoxical result of this analysis is that overall portfolio
risk is reduced by the addition of a small number of riskier foreign
securities. Because returns from foreign stocks are only moderately correlated with the returns from domestic stocks (remember, the correlation coefficient of the EAFE and S&P Indexes is
only about 0.5), some mixture of the two markets actually has
greater safety (less risk) than either set of securities alone. Good
returns from Japanese automakers, for example, balanced out
poor returns from domestic ones during a time when the Japanese share of the U.S. market increased. On the other hand, good
returns from U.S. manufacturing firms balanced out poor returns

from European manufacturers when the dollar became more competitive and Europe remained in a recession as the U.S. economy boomed. It is precisely these offsetting movements that reduced the overall volatility of the portfolio.

It turns out that the portfolio with the least risk had 30 percent foreign securities and 70 percent U.S. securities. Moreover, as Figure 6-1 shows, adding 30 percent EAFE stocks to a domestic portfolio also tended to increase portfolio return. In this sense, international diversification provided the closest thing to a free lunch available in our world securities markets. When higher portfolio returns can be achieved with lower risk by adding international stocks, no individual or institutional portfolio manager should fail to take notice.

International stocks will not always provide higher returns than U.S. stocks. During the eleven-year period covered by Figure 6-1, the EAFE return exceeded the return on the S&P 500. But such has not always been the case. For example, in 1996 the S&P 500 far outdistanced the stock markets of Europe and Japan. Nevertheless, the risk reduction benefits of diversification remain no matter which markets do best. As long as correlations among markets remain in less than a perfect lockstep relationship, investors will gain considerable benefits from international diversification.

Further Gains from Adding Emerging Markets

How do emerging markets fit into this overall scheme? The surprising answer is that they actually enrich the menu. Despite the fact that emerging stock markets are wildly volatile—having bucked up and down much more violently than the U.S. stock market—further diversification into these markets can actually give investors an opportunity to increase their returns while further reducing risk. We come very close to a situation where $100 bills are lying around just waiting to be picked up. Recall Markowitz's theory of optimal diversification: The lower the correlations between markets, the more risk reduction can be achieved.

Correlations between broad indexes of emerging-market stocks and the U.S. stock market are generally lower than those of the U.S. stock market with developed foreign markets. Correlation coefficients between emerging markets and the U.S. market are generally well below +0.5, and often below +0.25. Moreover, correlations between emerging-market returns and those of developed European and Asian markets are also low. This suggests that considerable further diversification benefits can be achieved by investors who expand their horizons to include stocks from all over the world. Most Americans are global consumers: they buy cars from Japan and Germany, television sets from Asia, and a variety of goods from emerging-market countries, from nearby Mexico to far-off Thailand. Just as consumers benefit from the global marketplace, so too can investors benefit from global investing.

Figure 6-2 shows the dramatic improvement in investment outcomes that has been achieved from the mid-1980s to the mid-1990s by diversification into emerging markets as well as foreign developed markets. The curve on the bottom is the same as the one in the preceding figure showing the diversification benefits of combining the S&P 500 Index with the EAFE Index. The new curve on the top shows the combinations of return and safety level available when emerging-market stocks from Asia, eastern Europe, and Latin America are added to the available set of possible investments. Remarkably, some addition of very risky emerging-market stocks actually increased safety levels (reduced risk) and provided a far more attractive menu of risk/return combinations than was available from the different portfolios of stocks from developed markets alone. It is also interesting to examine the portfolio that provided the least risk, or most safety. Note that this portfolio provided a higher return and lower risk than was possible without investing in emerging markets. The composition of the portfolio with the least risk included 61 percent U.S. common stocks, 26 percent stocks from the EAFE Index, and 13 percent emerging-markets securities. As an old Chinese proverb advises, "Sometimes there is safety in the most dangerous places."

FIGURE 6-2

**Adding Emerging Markets to the Portfolio
Provides Substantial Benefits for Investors**

Over an eleven-year period ending in 1995, the mix that provided
the highest return available with the least risk was 61% U.S. stocks,
26% developed-country stocks, and 13% emerging-market stocks.

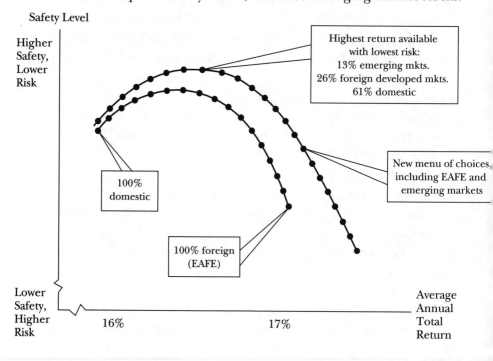

Diversification in the Future

Thus it has been possible to achieve greater returns and less risk
from a portfolio of common stocks drawn from both developed
economies and emerging markets. But while this combination
has, in fact, worked well in the past, one can legitimately question
whether it will work equally well in the future. We are reminded of
the correspondence between Isadora Duncan, the 1920s intellec-
tual flapper and doyenne of modern dance, and George Bernard

Shaw. Duncan wrote to Shaw proposing that they combine to produce a child, which, she argued, would be a model of perfection, combining his brains and her beauty. In Shavian fashion he declined her offer, suggesting, "Suppose it had your brains and looked like me?" Is it reasonable, then, to expect that a blend of worldwide securities will continue to yield a winning combination?

Many analysts feel that the globalization of the world economies has blunted the benefits of international diversification. They cite the fact that the October 1987 U.S. stock market crash appeared to turn the diversification argument on its head as stock markets around the world fell in sympathy with the U.S. market. Moreover, the collapse of the Mexican peso in 1995 had negative effects on almost all the emerging stock markets of the world. But while there is a tendency for short-run periods of stress to spread globally, careful research does not reveal a long-term trend toward increased correlation among world markets. The long-run evidence is that the correlations of national markets have remained quite low into the 1990s. To be sure, nations have become more closely linked by trade and the advance of instantaneous communications to the point where CNN is now heard even in Moscow and Beijing, making it likely that all markets will continue to respond to "global events." But even if correlations do increase somewhat in the future, investing in international, and especially emerging, markets will still be an important way of diversifying and therefore reducing risk.

Figure 6-3 shows how correlations between markets have behaved over time. The top panel shows the correlations of the EAFE Index with the S&P 500. Every three years a correlation coefficient between quarterly EAFE returns and U.S. stock returns was calculated, and the three-year correlation coefficients were plotted over time. On average, the correlation coefficient between EAFE and the S&P 500 Index was a little under 0.5. Note, however, that there has been no tendency for the correlations to rise over time. Indeed, during periods in the mid-1990s when the U.S. dollar strengthened against major foreign currencies and the U.S.

market soared, the correlations declined dramatically. Clearly, there is no support yet for the argument that globalization has a tendency to tie different national markets together more closely, and there is still ample opportunity for diversification to produce substantial benefits.

The bottom panel of the figure shows the correlations of the U.S. stock market with emerging markets. Note that these correlations tended to be considerably lower than was the case for developed markets. Correlation coefficients averaged approximately 0.35 with the emerging markets, thus providing even more substantial benefits from diversification, as illustrated opposite. Also note that the figures do not reveal any tendency for these correlations to increase over time. Indeed, the correlations in the period including the stock market crash of 1987 were generally much higher than the correlations for more recent periods. Even if they should eventually rise, there will still be considerable room for diversification to work its magic. Even if correlations with emerging markets doubled from their ten-year average, diversification would still provide tremendous benefits. All this evidence leads us to conclude that putting somewhere between 30 and 40 percent of a United States portfolio into international stocks is likely to decrease portfolio risk and possibly increase return. When emerging markets are combined with stocks in rich countries, investors obtain the next best thing to a free lunch: greater safety and a likelihood of higher returns.

Playing the Home Team

"Hold on!" some American portfolio manager naysayers may cry. They may suggest that it is not necessary to take the trouble to invest internationally since many U.S. corporations already do so. Why invest in local companies in lands you might hesitate to visit as a tourist when you can put your money into U.S.-headquartered companies that have overseas plants or subsidiaries? There is considerable merit to this argument and those who use it follow what

FIGURE 6-3

Correlations of Foreign Developed and Emerging Markets with the U.S. Stock Market

Developed Markets

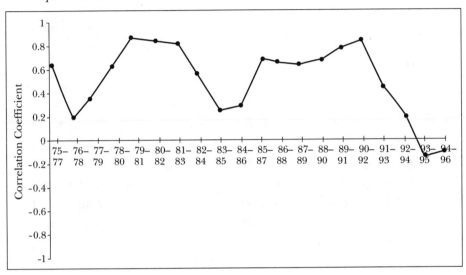

Emerging Markets

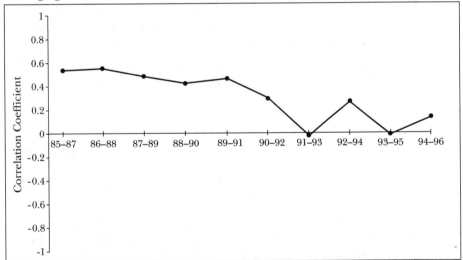

The points show the measured correlation coefficients for quarterly returns for various three-year periods from 1975 (for developed markets) and 1985 (for emerging markets) through 1996.

we call a "playing the home team" approach. Quite a few institutional investors use this strategy and say their portfolio is diversified because it includes significant holdings in American companies that have a large percentage of their sales and earnings in rapidly growing developing markets.

Procter & Gamble (P&G) is an excellent example of such a holding as it has had extraordinary success in foreign markets. In China alone, P&G has a 20 percent share of the growing laundry detergent market. If the average Chinese family doubles its spending on laundry detergent by the year 2000, P&G's soap sales in China will rise to more than $500 million! The company has also had considerable success in developing China's shampoo market. Dandruff is a common Chinese malady, and P&G's dandruff-controlling shampoo commands a 300 percent price premium over local brands. By running circles around the archaic state distribution system, P&G has destroyed the myth that China is not a national market.

Similar successes in emerging markets have been registered by consumer product companies such as Gillette, Coca-Cola, McDonald's, Wrigley, and others. The profit growth of most multinationals has been enhanced significantly by their exposure to emerging markets. Without question, a far more attractive set of risk/return possibilities is available to investors who diversify their portfolios across both multinational corporations and those doing a purely domestic business.

Figure 6-4 shows the alternative safety/return possibilities available to U.S. investors over the decade from the mid-1980s through the mid-1990s. The solid line shows the menu of safety/return choices if investments had been limited to companies whose entire business was within the United States. The dashed line shows the improvement resulting from adding multinationals to the portfolio. Further diversification enables an investor to achieve equivalent returns with *greater* safety and *lower* risk. Thus, the argument that some of the benefits from emerging-market investments can easily be captured simply by investing in home-team companies that do some portion of their business throughout the world is correct.

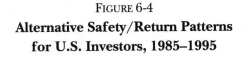

FIGURE 6-4

**Alternative Safety/Return Patterns
for U.S. Investors, 1985–1995**

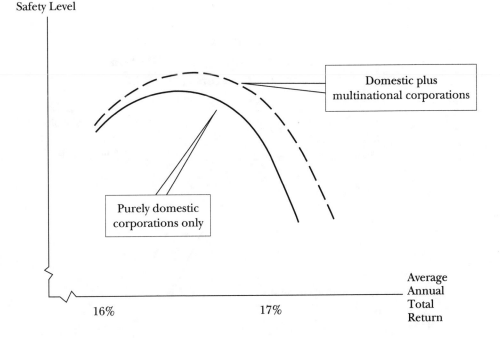

Unfortunately, the home-team strategy does not achieve all the benefits of investing directly in emerging markets because U.S. multinational corporations generally behave like other U.S. companies, even those doing a purely domestic business. When stock prices go up or down in general in the U.S. market, practically all companies follow suit. Recalling the discussion of portfolio theory earlier in this chapter, the evidence is that returns from all companies in the United States tend to be highly correlated with each other.

Much greater benefits from diversification can be achieved by investors willing to purchase stocks in emerging markets directly. This is illustrated in Figure 6-5, which presents results from the mid-1980s to the mid-1990s. It is the same as Figure 6-4 with the addition of a third dashed line, which includes portfolios made up not only of U.S. domestic and U.S. multinational corporations but also stocks of emerging-market corporations. We see that the

FIGURE 6-5

**Alternative Safety/Return Patterns
for U.S. Investors, 1985–1995**

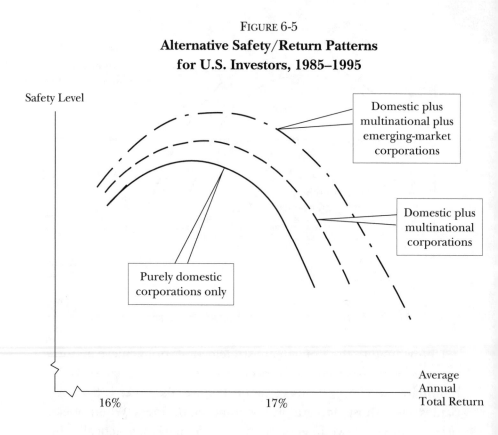

menu of choices available for investors is significantly enhanced by investing directly in emerging markets.

The reason this addition to the graph shows such a marked improvement over the other two portfolios is that emerging-market companies have far lower correlations with domestic U.S. companies than is the case for multinationals. Remember that the key to achieving the risk reduction benefits of diversification is to add assets to one's portfolio whose returns are *not* highly correlated with those already there. Only by directly purchasing stocks in emerging markets can the full benefits of emerging-market investing be achieved. To paraphrase a remark of a wealthy Texan, Clint Murchison, money is like manure: when you stack it up in concentrated piles, it stinks; when you spread it out widely over fields, it makes things grow. As attractive as the strategy of betting on the home team may appear, it fails to achieve the large benefits that are possible from purchasing emerging-market securities directly. In Part III, we present sensible and easy ways of implementing strategies that will enable investors to gain direct exposure to emerging-market securities.

PART II HIGHLIGHTS:

1. High return potentials in emerging markets come with high risks.

2. Many promising markets submerged in the past, shattering investors' dreams.

3. Political risk, market volatility, currency risks, high transactions costs, and lack of investor protection make emerging markets dangerous terrain for an unwary investor.

4. A knowledge of the history and characteristics of speculative excesses in emerging markets can protect investors from the most egregious errors.

5. The magic of diversification can substantially reduce investment risk. By building a diversified portfolio including both developed and emerging markets, investors can lower their portfolio risk and increase their return potentials.

PART III

HOW TO INVEST IN EMERGING MARKETS

GROWTH IS STIRRING in less developed markets throughout the world; the chapters in Part III tell you how to go about investing there. We present a variety of strategies from the safest and easiest methods of gaining emerging market exposure to the most daring and complex investment techniques, and we show the pros and cons of each alternative. In all instances, however, we have written this book for the nonprofessional investor. Anyone with an interest in investing can easily follow our advice.

In Chapter Seven we discuss managed investment funds that allow investors to purchase diversified portfolios of emerging-market securities. We explain the two main varieties of these funds—open-end and closed-end funds—and show how investors can choose between the two. We also present specific recommendations for individual investors.

Chapter Eight explains the pros and cons of perhaps the simplest method of investing in emerging markets—purchasing a single index fund that simply buys and holds a representative sample of companies in each emerging market. While this strategy has much to recommend it, it is not possible to find a completely adequate index that does the trick. For this reason, we suggest that an index strategy may need to be augmented, and we detail the steps investors need to take to obtain adequate diversification.

In Chapter Nine, we cover a far more complex and difficult

strategy—the direct purchase of individual securities in different emerging markets. While this strategy is suitable only for the most sophisticated investors with substantial resources, many investors will find the game of trying to discover the new Wal-Marts or Microsofts or the next Taiwan or Singapore of the world just too much fun to resist. This chapter offers some tips that may tilt the odds in your favor or at least help to contain the major risks involved.

Chapter Ten indicates investment opportunities in assets other than stocks. While most investors find that augmenting a developed-country domestic portfolio with emerging-market stocks provides the right investment mix, those with substantial assets may find an all-inclusive luxury tour more suitable. Here we explain investment opportunities in emerging-market debt, real estate, and natural resources.

Chapter Eleven presents some final travel tips that may be helpful as you start off on an exciting and enriching global bargain hunt.

CHAPTER SEVEN

The Professionally Managed Approach

UNLESS YOU HAVE the kind of money that would justify flying to Nairobi or Bangkok to investigate individual companies, you should probably do your hunting with the pros and use one or more investment funds as your vehicle for buying into emerging markets. These funds offer single-digit millionaires and people of modest means many benefits, including convenient diversification, freedom from having to select individual stocks, relief from the paperwork and record keeping necessary for tax purposes, and automatic reinvestment of any dividends.

The first, of course, is the most important benefit with regard to investing in emerging markets. Most people simply cannot afford to buy the broad number of country and regional stocks required to ensure adequate diversification. Not only is the sheer number of stocks required expensive to buy, so too are the commission costs on small purchases, many of which are enormous on overseas exchanges.

There are literally hundreds of emerging-market investment funds available, each touting its lures to obtain your investment dollar. We have split them into two categories: professionally managed funds and indexed, or computer-generated, funds.

Types of Professionally Managed Funds

As the name implies, professionally managed funds hire individuals to select the stocks in their portfolios. Appropriately known as fund managers, these people work with two basic forms of funds: the well-known open-end and the less known closed-end varieties. Open-end funds issue and redeem shares daily at current net asset values (NAVs), figured by dividing the total value of all the securities owned by the fund by the number of outstanding fund shares. Often known as "mutual funds," they are open in the sense that their size can increase or decrease according to demand. The more money people invest in a fund, the more shares are issued.

Closed-end funds, on the other hand, are finite. On their creation, a fixed number of shares is issued and set afloat in the marketplace. They are somewhat similar to corporation stocks in that if you wish to buy or sell shares after a closed-end fund has begun operation, you must do so on a securities exchange. Thus, the market price of a closed-end fund may deviate from its NAV, selling sometimes at a premium (above its NAV) and at other times at a discount (below its NAV). The premium, or discount, comes into play because the prices of closed-end funds are subject to the emotional pushes and pulls visited on stocks by securities markets. Sometimes investors love a closed-end fund so much that they will pay more than its NAV to obtain it. At other times, they will do anything to dump their holdings and will willingly sell them at less than their NAV.

Although it appears that closed-end funds suffer a price disadvantage because they are subject to the fickle whims of the marketplace, they have certain advantages over open-end funds and are particularly suitable for making money in emerging markets. One advantage is that closed-end funds have more control over the timing of their purchases and sales of securities. Remember, open-end funds are just that. When stocks are climbing through the roof and subject to excessive speculative optimism, investors tend to pour money in—and the managers are forced to boost their holdings at prices that are being driven up by the surplus of money. When the inevitable correction sets in and prices fall, investors often pull their money out and fund managers find themselves selling during market lows to raise cash for these redemptions, meanwhile bemoaning the fact that there is little cash available to scoop up bargains at reduced prices. Managers of closed-end funds, on the other hand, do not have to deal with being forced to buy at the top and sell at the bottom. This aspect of closed-end funds is a money saver when dealing with emerging-market shares because, as mentioned earlier, the transactions costs of buying and selling these shares are quite large.

One of the best available sources of information about both open- and closed-end funds is the Morningstar mutual fund information service. On a single page, Morningstar presents a full summary of all the information an investor needs to know about a fund. It shows the portfolio's composition, its past returns, its risk level, and information on sales charges (if any) and expenses. Morningstar also presents a star rating system, with five stars representing the best. A fund receives a higher number of stars if its past performance is good and risk level is low. A fund is downgraded, even if its past returns have been good, if its risk level or expense level is high. Since we tend to be averse to high risk and high expenses, we like the Morningstar system. But unlike the Michelin dining guide, whose stars are a reliable predictor of how well a diner will eat, the Morningstar ratings are not a guarantee of superior performance. Five-star funds do not reliably outperform one-star funds, and therefore investors should not select funds solely on the basis of their star rating. A sample Morningstar rating sheet for the open-end T. Rowe Price New Asia Stock Fund is shown on the following page.

In addition to Morningstar, the Herzfeld organization is an excellent source of information on closed-end funds. The "Herzfeld Guide to Closed-End Funds" presents useful information on historical discounts and offers advice consistent with our own "buy the deep discounts" philosophy, which we will describe below.

Fund Detail	Page 1 of 1		Release Date: 05-31-96

T. Rowe Price New Asia

	Rating ★★	Manager Name Management Team	Objective Pacific Stock

Investment Approach

Equity Style

Value Blend Growth

Large	Size: —
Medium	Style: —
Small	

Fixed-Income Style

Short Int Long

High	Quality: —
Medium	Maturity: —
Low	

Portfolio Profile

Composition % assets 03-31-96   **Turnover**

Cash	6.7	64 %
Stocks*	91.3	
Bonds	0.0	**12 Month Yield**
Other	2.1	0.99 %
*Foreign	98.2	
(% of stocks)		

Sector Weightings % stocks 10-31-95

🔌	Utilities	8.1
🔥	Energy	1.0
💲	Financials	50.1
⚙	Cyclicals	14.0
🍎	Durables	6.7
🍸	Staples	1.9
⚒	Services	13.6
🛒	Retail	1.1
✚	Health	0.4
💻	Technology	3.1

Risk / Return Profile

	Morningstar Risk	Morningstar Return
3 Yr	High	Below Avg
5 Yr	High	Average
10 Yr	—	—

Avg Hist Rating Over 33 Mos:3.5★s

MPT Statistics Relative to S&P 500

R-Squared	3 Yr	24
Beta	3 Yr	1.42
Alpha	3 Yr	-7.47

Bear Market Performance

Decile Rank within Investment Objective —
1 = Best 10%; 10 = Worst 10%

Trailing Period Performance

	YTD	1 Mo	3 Mo	12 Mo	3Yr Annlzd	5Yr Annlzd	10Yr Annlzd	15Yr Annlzd
Total Return %	10.46	-1.73	-0.22	7.49	11.53	12.90	—	—
± S&P 500	0.79	-4.30	-5.31	-20.92	-5.64	-1.65	—	—
± MS Pcf	7.84	2.61	-3.84	0.37	6.64	7.34	—	—
Decile Rank within Investment Objective	2	6	10	8	3	2	—	—
1=Best 10%; 10=Worst 10%								
Load-Adjusted Return%				7.49		12.90		

Growth of $10,000 from 10-01-90 to 05-31-96

— T. Rowe Price New Asia $ 22,347

— Pacific Stock $ 19,226

— S&P 500 $ 25,731

Calendar Year Performance

	1986	1987	1988	1989	1990	1991	1992	1993	1994	1995	5-96
Total Return %	—	—	—	—	—	19.32	11.24	78.76	-19.15	3.75	10.46
± S&P 500	—	—	—	—	—	-11.16	3.62	68.70	-20.47	-33.78	0.79
± MS Pcf	—	—	—	—	—	8.02	29.64	43.07	-31.98	0.97	7.84

Operations

Ticker:	PRASX	Minimum Initial Purchase:	$2500	Front-End Fees:	0.00 %
Family:	Price T. Rowe Funds	Minimum IRA Purchase:	$1000	Deferred Load	0.00 %
Inception:	09-90	Minimum Auto Invstmnt Plan:	$50	12b-1 Fee	0.00 %
Manager:	Management Team	Purchase Constraints:	—	Expense Ratio:	1.15 %
Tenure:	6 Years	Shareholder Report Grade:	A	Assets:	$2369.2 mil 04-30-96
Telephone:	800-638-5660			NAV:	9.08

MORNINGSTAR   Ascent™

Paying Full Price and More for Open-End Funds

Since most funds are of the open-end variety, we will examine this category first. With thousands of such funds available, competition for the investor's dollar is keen. Many funds try to beat a path to investors' doors by hiring salespeople to tout their advantages. New customers, not the fund, pay for these sales pitches through a commission that is tacked onto the fund's NAV sales price. Funds that employ commissioned sales forces, such as stockbrokers and insurance agents, are known as "load funds"; and those that do not are called "no-load funds," or "no-loads."

In our opinion, buying a load fund is the equivalent of stepping up to bat with two strikes already against you. Your investment has to earn enough money to cover the load, or commission cost, before it can even begin to work for you. And funds are very tricky in describing how hard they will hit you with these commissions. Some load fees, for example, are publicly stated as being as high as 8.5 percent. Thus, a reasonable person would assume that if she bought a share worth $10 in such a fund, she would pay an extra $.85 in load fees. Not so: she would actually pay $.93! The fund comes up with an 8.5 percent commission figure by dividing the *total* cost of $10.93 by the $.93 sales charge—very tricky.

No-load funds tend to be a bit more straightforward. With few or no direct-sales personnel, they will not usually knock at your door; in general, you have to call them. Since they sell at their NAV, you would pay only $10 for a share with an NAV of $10 (as opposed to the $10.93 in the above example). Do not, however, think that you are free of sales costs. Many "no-load" funds impose 12B-1 charges, which are annual fees that help defray the selling expenses of the fund. The investor does not pay a load per se, but selling expenses reduce net asset value and thus are taken out of the investor's hide year after year. Open-end investors should look for funds that have neither loads nor 12B-1 charges. Also, funds that charge large redemption fees should be avoided.

Listed in Table 7-1 is a group of some of the best-known open-end funds investing in emerging markets. We prefer the no-load funds on the list and in general favor those with lower annual expense ratios. We also like funds with relatively low turnover (percentage of portfolio changed during a year) because buying and selling in illiquid emerging markets involves large transactions costs as well as capital gains liabilities. The funds in Table 7-1 generally meet these criteria. For completeness, four of the better-known load funds are also included in the table.

The funds in the top half of the table are widely diversified funds. They invest in most emerging countries and in all regions. While the funds may from time to time overweight various sectors where the fund managers believe the best investment prospects and fairest prices lie, any of the funds listed would provide an adequate representation of emerging-market common stocks with a single one-stop-shopping instrument. The funds listed at the bottom of the table are also diversified, but they invest in particular regions rather than over the whole world.

One warning about mutual funds is in order. Be very careful about rushing into a fund simply because it has an excellent recent record. As we have warned repeatedly, emerging markets are extremely volatile, and a spectacular past run is not a reliable guide that similar returns will accrue in the future. When a fund's advertisements trumpet extraordinary recent performance, take that as a hint that you should be more cautious rather than more enthusiastic about investing in it.

Finding Buried Treasure Among Closed-End Funds

Recall that closed-end funds may sell at a discount to their NAV. That happened when the Mexican currency crisis rippled through all emerging markets and created the so-called Tequila Effect. Investors panicked, and anything associated with emerging-market investments, particularly closed-end funds, took a nosedive. The closed-end funds were especially hard hit because investors were so anxious to dump them that they sold their shares well below the underlying NAV. Many discounts exceeded 20 percent, making such funds "negative-load" funds.

TABLE 7-1

Sample of Open-End Emerging-Market Funds

Fund	Morning-star Rating	Load Fee (%)	Expense Ratio (%/year)	Turn-over (%)	Return 1996 (%)	Net Assets 1996 (in millions)	Minimum Investment Required	Telephone Number
Widely diversified funds:								
Fidelity Emerging Markets	2	3.00	1.28	78	10	$1,497	$2,500	(800) 544-8888
Montgomery Emerging Markets	NA	0	1.80	92	12	997	1,000	(800) 572-3863
Robertson Stephens Developing Countries	NA	0	1.83	NA	21	35	5,000	(800) 766-3863
SSgA Emerging Markets	NA	0	1.50	20	15	109	1,000	(800) 647-7327
Templeton Developing Markets	2	5.75	2.10	21	23	2,835	100	(800) 292-9293
T. Rowe Price Emerging Markets	NA	0	1.75	69	12	51	2,500	(800) 638-5660
Warburg Pincus Emerging Markets	NA	0	1.00	31	10	187	2,500	(800) 927-2874
Regional funds:								
Colonial Newport Tiger	4	5.75	1.49	4	11	207	1,000	(800) 248-2828
T. Rowe Price New Asia	2	0	1.15	64	14	2,369	2,500	(800) 638-5660
Fidelity Latin America	1	3.00	1.41	57	31	620	2,500	(800) 544-8888

SOURCE: Morningstar; *Barron's.*

While the Tequila Effect was a particularly dramatic occurrence, closed-end funds more often than not sell at a discount. Why this is so is something of a puzzle. We have mentioned that discounts appear to rise and fall with general market sentiment. But why, on average, have these funds tended to sell at less than their NAVs while their open-end brethren do not? We believe that the answer lies in the lack of sales incentives for brokers and fund-management companies. Remember that once a closed-end fund is sold to the public, the manager of the fund collects fees on the basis of the fund's assets, not its market price. Since no new shares are being offered, the manager has no incentive to spend money on advertising or otherwise promoting the shares. Moreover, stockbrokers earn more money promoting and selling open-end fund shares with substantial sales charges (load fees). For example, a securities salesman (broker) might earn a commission of $300 selling a customer $10,000 worth of an open-end fund with a 6 percent load fee. (The salesman might receive about half of the $600 [6 percent] load fee as a commission.) But if that same broker sold $10,000 worth of a closed-end fund, a normal brokerage commission might come to about $200, and the typical earnings of the broker would be only about $60 (30 percent of the total). Thus, brokers prefer to sell open-end funds to the public and are less likely to be enthusiastic supporters of closed-end fund shares.

You can often profit handsomely from this brokerage neglect. Recall that when a closed-end fund is selling at a discount, you can purchase the full asset value at a bargain price. Thus, when the discount is at 15 percent, you can buy a $10 NAV share for only $8.50. It is these discounts that give closed-end funds a special attraction. *Whenever you can buy assets at discounts of 15 percent, 20 percent, or more, it is usually time to open your wallet to closed-end funds.*

At the start of 1997, many closed-end funds were available at discounts of nearly 20 percent, close to the lowest level since Saddam Hussein bombed the market in 1990. If these discounts were to narrow or even be eliminated in the future, investors could make attractive returns even if the net asset value of funds remain constant. Moreover, even if the discount remained constant, investors will find that they will earn returns exceeding the returns from the fund's assets. A simple illustration will make the advantage clear. Suppose a fund with an NAV of $10 per share is selling at a 20 percent discount, at $8 per share. Assume that over a period of time, the market moves up and the fund's NAV doubles. The fund has returned $10 in capital appreciation, which is usually paid out over time in the form of capital gains distributions, leaving the stated NAV at $10.

If the discount does not change, the fund will continue selling at $8. The investor's return at that point will be 125 percent ($10 capital gains distributions divided by $8 purchase price), substantially better than the 100 percent total return on the fund's assets. Any dividend yield the fund pays will similarly be magnified. Suppose the dividend paid by the fund is $0.50 per year, or 5 percent of NAV. Based on a purchase price of $8, the dividend yield received by the investor is 6.25 percent. Remember that on every distribution the fund makes, whether dividend or capital gains earnings, the investor receives the whole amount—there is no discount.

Although we have some doubts about the efficacy of active management of a portfolio of publicly traded securities, many of the managers of closed-end funds do have reputations for being the most skilled in the business. Mark Mobius, who runs the Templeton Emerging Markets Funds, is one of the best known and most visible, partly due to his uncanny resemblance to the late Yul Brynner. A workaholic dedicated to spending every waking moment in the search for bargain stocks all over the developing world, Mobius has racked up an unusually strong performance record. Other than taking time out for a one-hour jog at dawn and a visit to a health club late at night, he spends his time tracking down growth opportunities for investors and has earned a well-deserved reputation as an investment superstar. In his own Gulfstream jet, Mobius spends hundreds of days each year jetting around the world to check on his investments. Similarly, Morgan Stanley's urbane chief strategist, Barton Biggs, and his emerging-markets guru, Madhav Dhar (a man who got his job at Morgan Stanley by offering to work for no salary), have earned an enviable worldwide reputation. The point is that while closed-end funds can be thought of as bargain-basement investments, the talent running the funds is as good as any in the world.

Nevertheless, despite the periodic attractiveness of deep discounts and fund management that is as good as that of open-end funds, it is important to remember that the discounts on closed-end funds are very volatile. When investors are particularly optimistic about emerging markets in general and one country or region in particular, a fund may sell at a substantial premium. When investors are pessimistic, it may sell at a substantial discount. Figure 7-1 illustrates the extraordinary volatility of discounts and premiums for the Latin America Equity Fund. In early 1994, it sold at a 15 percent premium. Later in the decade, after the Tequila Effect, it sold at a substantial discount. The following rules will help you profit the most from this kind of volatile—but rewarding—investment.

Some General Rules for Buyers of Closed-End Funds

1. *Never buy a closed-end fund at a premium.* Because closed-end funds tend, on average, to sell at a discount, it is unwise in most circumstances ever to pay more than NAV for a closed-end fund, especially when open-end funds are available at NAV. If a fund swings from a 10 percent premium to a 10 percent discount (roughly the long-run average discount for these funds), the resulting loss of capital will be 18 percent. This loss will be compounded further if the fund's NAV goes down as well. Unless there are restrictions on investments in a particular country and a closed-end fund is the only way of participating, always avoid paying a premium. Even where there are restrictions causing the premium, we advise passing up the fund. In the future, the restrictions are likely to be lifted as the developing country seeks capital, and the premium is likely to melt away.

2. *Never buy a closed-end fund at its initial offering price.* A corollary to Rule 1 is never to buy a closed-end fund when it is first offered

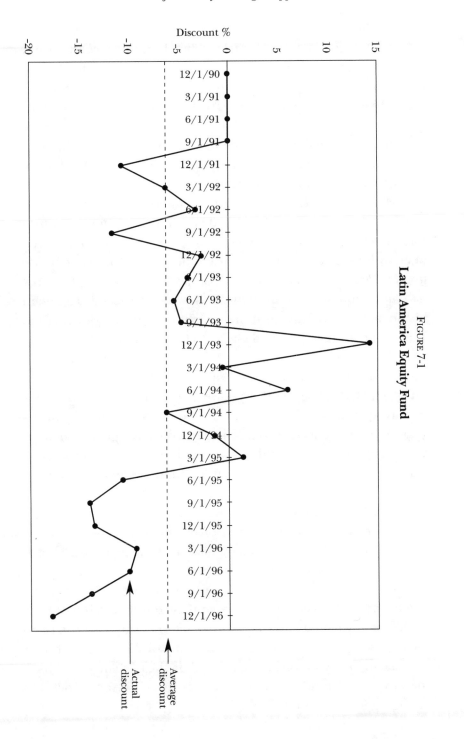

FIGURE 7-1
Latin America Equity Fund

to the public. Brokers will often suggest to their clients that the investor gets a good deal on initial public offerings since they carry no commission. Actually, an underwriting and selling fee of perhaps 7 percent is built into the initial offering price. That means that if an investor pays $10 per share, the fund receives only $9.30. Thus, the investor is paying $1 for 93 cents of assets, or an effective premium of more than 7.5 percent. Moreover, funds usually go to a discount soon after their initial public offering. Initial public offerings of closed-end shares are usually a rip-off.

3. *Always buy a closed-end fund at an attractive discount.* Insist on substantial discounts on the closed-end funds you buy. For funds traded in the United States, you can check current discounts each week by looking at the weekly edition of *Barron's,* the Sunday edition of *The New York Times* or the Monday edition of *The Wall Street Journal.* A sample discount table is shown in Table 7-2. To obtain historical average discount information, consult Morningstar, Value Line, or the "Herzfeld Guide to Closed-End Funds."

4. *Look for low expense ratios and low turnover.* As with open-end funds, you should favor funds with low expense ratios and low turnover. High expenses drag down the net returns available for the investor, and high turnover tends to reduce returns by incurring high transactions costs and increased capital gains liabilities. While expense ratios tend to be relatively high for emerging-market funds, we recommend that if a fund has an expense ratio of more than 2 percent per year, it should be avoided.

5. *Buy through discount brokers.* Remember that in purchasing a closed-end fund, you will incur a brokerage commission. We advise that you make your purchase charge as inexpensive as possible. The best policy is to use a discount broker or negotiate a low rate with a full-service broker. Almost everything in life is negotiable, and commissions are no exception. You should buy at least $2,000 of any closed-end fund you select to ensure that the commission is kept below 1.5 percent of your investment. You should also ensure that your order is executed on the exchange on which the closed-end fund is traded (such as the New York Stock Exchange). Some discount brokers will charge very low, or even no,

TABLE 7-2
Premiums and Discounts
on Selected Closed-End Funds, May 2, 1997
World Equity Funds*

Fund Name (Symbol)	Net Asset Value	Market Price	Premium (+) Discount (−)
Argentina (AF)	15.15	13 ¼	−12.5
Asia Pacific (APB)	13.77	11 ⅜	−17.4
Asia Tigers (GRR)	12.79	10 ½	−17.9
Brazil (BZF)	31.52	25 ¾	−18.3
Brazilian Equity (BZL)	19.27	15 ½	−19.6
Cdn Genl Inv (CGI)	17.45	13 ⁵¹⁄₆₄	−20.9
Chile (CH)	26.98	24 ⅝	−8.7
China (CHN)	18.71	15 ⅛	−19.2
Czech Republic (CRF)	15.15	13 ½	−10.9
Emer Mkts Grow (N/A)	62.89	N/A	N/A
Emerging Mexico (MEF)	9.44	7 ⅜	−21.9
F&C Middle East (EME)	20.22	17 ¼	−14.7
Fidelity Em Asia (FAE)	15.92	13 ½	−15.2
Fidelity Ad Korea (FAK)	8.07	7 ⅞	−2.4
First Iberian (IBF)	14.74	11 ⅜	−22.8
First Israel (ISL)	15.70	12 ¾	−18.8
First Philippine (FRF)	15.91	13 ⅝	−14.4
GT Devel Mkts (GTD)	14.63	11 ⅞	−18.8
GT Glbl Estn Eur (GTF)	17.65	14 ¾	−16.4
Greater China (GCH)	21.17	16 ⅝	−21.5
Herzfeld Caribb (CUBA)	5.70	5	−12.3
India Fund (IFN)	8.85	8 ⅝	−2.5
India Growth (IGF)	11.41	12 ¼	+7.4
Indonesia (IF)	10.85	10 ⅛	−6.7
Jakarta Growth (JGF)	10.02	8 ⅝	−13.9
Jardine Fl China (JFC)	16.16	12 ⅝	−21.9
Jardine Fl India (JFI)	9.22	8 ¾	−5.1
Korea (KF)	12.30	12 ⅞	+4.7
Korea Equity (KEF)	6.09	6 ⅛	+0.6
Korean Inv (KIF)	7.51	7 ⅛	−5.1

World Equity Funds*

Fund Name (Symbol)	Net Asset Value	Market Price	Premium (+) Discount (−)
Latin Amer Disc (LDF)	18.36	16 ⅛	−12.2
Latin Amer Eq (LAQ)	18.29	15 ⅝	−14.6
Latin Amer Growth (LLF)	13.12	10 ⅞	−17.1
Latin Amer Inv (LAM)	21.33	17 ⅝	−17.4
Malaysia (MF)	17.01	15	−11.8
Mexico (MXF)	20.07	16	−20.3
Mexico Eqty&Inc (MXE)	12.91	10 ¼	−20.6
Morgan St Africa (AFF)	20.99	17	−19.0
Morgan St Asia (APF)	12.09	9 ⅞	−18.3
Morgan St Em (MSF)	18.42	16 ⅛	−12.5
Morgan St India (IIF)	10.61	11	+3.7
Morgan St Russia (RNE)	27.99	24 ½	−12.5
New South Africa (NSA)	18.22	14 ⅝	−19.7
Pakistan Inv (PKF)	5.57	5 ¼	−5.7
Portugal (PGF)	20.03	16 ⅜	−18.2
ROC Taiwan (ROC)	14.90	12 ⅛	−18.6
Schroder Asian (SHF)	12.87	11 ⅜	−11.6
Scudder New Asia (SAF)	15.25	12 ⅞	−15.6
Scudder New Eur (NEF)	18.44	15	−18.7
Singapore (SGF)	11.96	10 ⅞	−9.1
Southern Africa (SOA)	20.50	16 ¾	−18.3
TCW/DW Emer Mkts (EMO)	14.99	13 ⅝	−9.1
Taiwan (TWN)	31.26	25	−20.0
Taiwan Equity (TYW)	15.50	11 ¾	−24.2
Templeton China (TCH)	16.25	13	−20.0
Templeton Dragon (TDF)	19.28	15 ⅛	−21.6
Templeton Em App (TEA)	15.36	13 ⅜	−12.9
Templeton Em Mkt (EMF)	19.96	20 ¾	+4.0
Templeton Russia (TRF)	32.12	31 ⅛	−3.1
Templeton Vietnm (TVF)	14.22	11 ⅝	−18.2
Thai (TTF)	13.26	15 ⅜	+16.0
Thai Capital (TC)	7.86	8 ⅞	+12.9
Turkish Inv (TKF)	5.89	5 ⅝	−4.5

*Only funds invested in emerging-market securities are included.

World Income Funds*

Fund Name (Symbol)	Net Asset Value	Market Price	Premium (+) Discount (−)
Americas Inc Tr (XUS)	8.97	7 ½	−16.4
Emer Mkts Float (EFL)	16.58	17	+2.5
Emer Mkts Inc (EMD)	19.87	17 ½	−11.9
Emer Mkts Inc II (EDF)	16.59	15 ½	−6.6
Lat Am $ Income (LBF)	16.22	14 ⅞	−8.3
Morg St Em Debt (MSD)	14.75	13 ⅝	−7.6
Templeton Em Inc (TEI)	13.75	12 ¾	−7.3

*Only funds invested in emerging-market securities are included.

commissions but will sell you shares from their inventories at inflated prices so that the transaction is actually more expensive than if you used a full-service broker to begin with. Our advice is to put your orders in as "limit orders," where you specify the price you are willing to pay, thus ensuring that the order price you give entails buying the shares at an attractive discount from NAV.

6. *Adopt a buy-and-hold strategy.* Be prepared to own the fund for at least five years, and do not trade from fund to fund. Buying and holding minimizes transactions costs and taxes. You should also consider signing up for a dividend reinvestment program, which uses your dividends and capital gains distributions to buy more shares at discounted market prices. Most funds and brokers have plans available that enable investors to use their dividends to purchase more shares with either low or no transactions charges.

Choosing Particular Closed-End Funds

Closed-end funds concentrating in emerging-market equities come in three categories: (1) diversified funds investing in all emerging markets; (2) regional funds investing in particular regions of the world; and (3) individual country funds. Investors

TABLE 7-3

Closed-End Funds at Attractive Discounts, January 1997

Fund	Morningstar Rating	January 1997 Price (U.S.$)	NAV (U.S.$)	Discount (%)*	Average Discount Since 1990 (%) (Premium)
Diversified funds:					
Morgan Stanley Emerging Markets	3	16	17.18	6.9	(5.0)
Templeton Emerging Markets	5	20⅛	19.40	(3.7)	(13.4)
Regional funds:					
Czech Republic Fund	NA	14½	16.56	12.4	6.5
Scudder New Asia	3	13⅜	15.64	14.5	2.7
Latin America Equity Fund	2	15½	17.89	13.4	4.0
Schroder Asian Growth	NA	12¼	13.64	10.2	2.7
Templeton Dragon	NA	15⅝	19.08	18.1	11.0
Morgan Stanley Africa	NA	14⅜	18.69	23.1	18.0
Country funds:					
First Philippine	4	16⅜	20.21	19.0	18.3
Mexico Fund	3	16⅜	19.78	17.2	5.3
Thai Fund	4	16⅝	14.86	(11.9)	(0.5)
India Fund	NA	8¼	7.86	(5.0)	10.3
Malaysia Fund	3	17⅞	19.35	7.6	1.4
Brazil Fund	5	23⅛	27.52	16.0	0.1
Chile Fund	5	22⅛	24.68	10.4	6.6
Korea Fund	4	16¾	14.42	(16.2)	(22.0)
ROC Taiwan Fund	2	10⅞	12.53	13.2	(0.2)

*(Number in parenthesis indicates premium)

Expense Ratio (%)	Turnover (%)	Performance, 1990–1996 (annual rate of return)	Remarks	Telephone Number
1.75	52	NA	Run by Barton Biggs and Madhav Dhar	(800) 221-6726
1.73	28	24.02	Run by Mark Mobius	(800) 292-9293
1.91	52	NA	Also invests in other eastern European countries such as Hungary and Poland	(800) 421-4777
1.67	82	11.53	A highly rated Asia fund	(800) 349-4281
1.70	78	NA	Relatively moderate expense ratio for the region	(212) 832-2626
1.08	62	NA	Fund required to offer buy shares at NAV if discount too large	(800) 688-0928
1.54	NA	NA	A good window into China	(800) 292-9293
1.87	NA	25.40	Largest African fund	(800) 221-6726
1.82	21	19.86	Only Philippine fund rated by Morningstar	(800) 524-4458
1.14	11	9.43	Low expense ratio	(800) 224-4134
1.22	22	24.62	Run by Morgan Stanley	(617) 557-8000
NA	NA	NA	Largest India fund	(800) 421-4777
1.19	23	16.56	Run by Morgan Stanley	(617) 557-8000
1.71	6	36.05	Top-rated Brazil fund	(800) 349-4281
1.39	1	34.57	Top-rated Chile fund	(212) 832-2626
1.32	11	6.46	Best vehicle for Korean investment	(800) 349-4281
1.98	81	3.75	Best vehicle for Taiwan investment	(800) 343-9567

with limited assets will probably be best served by purchasing one of the diversified funds. Investors of more substantial means may wish to purchase a portfolio of regional funds, perhaps augmented with funds specializing in particular countries. We show later that country and regional funds can also play an important role in helping to fill out an "indexed" portfolio (described in Chapter Eight) so that it is adequately diversified.

The general selection rules are the same as those for open-end funds. Investors should seek funds with relatively low expenses and turnover. In addition, we recommend that investors purchase a fund only at a discount that is at least as large as its historical average. Table 7-3 lists the average discount since 1990 as well as the January 1997 discount for a number of funds, many of which remained attractively priced throughout 1997. The table also gives other pertinent information.

Taking Risks—and Profits—with Closed-End Funds Traded Abroad

While the closed-end funds listed in Table 7-3 all trade in New York, there are many others that can be bought only overseas in markets located in major cities, such as Bangkok, Hong Kong, London, Luxembourg, and Singapore. Many of these funds are available at even larger discounts than those available in the New York markets. While discounts on the U.S. market may reach 15 or 20 percent, discounts on lower-profile exchanges have been known to reach 30 to 40 percent, as was the case in the early 1990s with several closed-end India funds listed in the United Kingdom. To be sure, the risks are larger since you could get ripped off by a dishonest foreign broker and you won't have the U.S. Securities and Exchange Commission looking over the fund's shoulder to protect you from scams. But with their substantially larger discounts, their risks could be worthwhile for sophisticated investors.

You should be aware that there are often good reasons for the large discount differentials among funds traded in different countries. The first is liquidity. For instance, while in the United States the existence of 2,000 investors is required to list a fund, the number of investors required to launch a fund in the United Kingdom could be fewer than 200. As a result, some funds traded in Britain are much less liquid. Second, the discount differentials may reflect a difference in expense ratios. Expense ratios for actively managed emerging-market funds vary from 1 percent to 3.7 percent, with overseas funds generally having higher expenses. While a high expense ratio may reflect more research effort and due diligence, there is little evidence that expenses are correlated with fund performance. Third, high commission costs as a result of excessive trading (which is not reflected in the stated expense ratio) may also reduce fund returns. Fourth, the NAV may not accurately reflect the true conversion value of the fund's portfolio because some of the funds may have very illiquid holdings. Fifth, different funds may have quite different risk profiles. As a result, investors may, in certain instances, take more risk when they substitute a U.S.-listed fund with one listed only in London or Hong Kong. Finally, and perhaps most important, there are very unfavorable tax effects for U.S. investors who buy foreign funds. U.S. taxpayers are liable for U.S. taxes on all income and realized gains in foreign funds, whether they are distributed or not. In addition, a severe interest penalty accumulates on any unpaid tax. We suggest that any closed-end funds listed only on foreign exchanges be placed only in IRAs or other tax-exempt investment vehicles.

As a result of these differences, investors should be aware that there could be persistent discount differentials among emerging-market funds in different countries. If the differentials persist over time and there has been some research suggesting that this is the case, investors may not be able to capture arbitrage profits by simultaneously selling low-discount funds and purchasing equivalent funds with higher discounts.

There are times, however, when investors in one market become overly pessimistic, relative to investors in other markets, about a region's prospects. Their pessimism could drive the normal discount spread to unusually high levels. This may create an attractive arbitrage opportunity for a sophisticated investor, who may buy a fund with a high discount and sell short a similar fund with a low discount. If the discount spread reverts to its normal level, the arbitrageur could earn a sizable profit.

A number of foreign funds have fixed termination dates (when the investor can be assured of getting out at NAV). For example, the Hungarian Investment Company and the Thailand International Fund both trade in London at substantial discounts and terminate in 1998. Other funds have provisions whereby if the fund continues to trade at a substantial discount, the fund must either make a tender offer for shares at NAV or bring a vote before the shareholders recommending that the fund be open-end. You should know, however, that closed-end fund managers invariably resist such open-end provisions since they fear they would lead to a loss of assets and thus a loss of income for the managers. Nevertheless, even if the discount does not narrow, investors will still obtain a higher rate of return on closed-end funds at big discounts than on open-end funds selling at NAV.

If you do attempt to purchase foreign closed-end funds, we recommend that you *not* use a discount broker. Here it will be wise to use a broker who has specialized knowledge in the closed-end fund area and broad global experience in dealing with foreign securities markets. Some firms that meet these criteria are Smith Barney, Morgan Stanley (Dean Witter, Discover), and Merrill Lynch. You are more likely to avoid mistakes by dealing with professionals who know their way around these global marketplaces. Current discount information for closed-end funds traded in London and Hong Kong is published in the *Financial Times* and *South China Morning Post*. The information is also available from Bloomberg, Dow Jones, and Micropal. Those with access to the Internet can also find performance information on closed-end funds worldwide on Lipper Analytical Service's site at http://www.lipperweb.com. Lipper tracks 18,000 closed- and open-end funds worldwide with total assets of approximately $3.6 trillion.

CHAPTER EIGHT

The Indexed, or Computer-Managed, Approach

HERE IS A statement that constitutes rank heresy within the investment community: The simplest way to choose the consistently most profitable portfolio of emerging-market stocks is to adopt an indexing approach. Most investment professionals say there is no such thing as simplicity. Indeed, they would probably agree with the comment of historian Henry Brooks Adams that "Simplicity is the most deceitful mistress that ever betrayed man." (Adams, it should be noted, wrote in pre–politically correct times.)

Actually, the investment community's wrath against simplicity is not so much that it is deceitful as that it is boring. And in a way, indexing is denigrating in that it ignores the millions of dollars spent on MBA degrees and the thousands of IQ points that go into determining how best to pick stocks. As far as indexes are concerned, bright, educated people do not count; mindless, number-crunching computers do.

What is this feared, hated creature called an "emerging-market index fund"? It is an open-end mutual fund that buys a representative sample of common stocks available for foreign investors in the world's developing markets and then simply holds the portfolio, making no attempt to trade from security to security or country to country in the hope of capturing particularly attractive investment opportunities. Because of its passive investment style, it minimizes transactions costs and taxes and can be managed far less expensively than an actively managed fund. While actively managed funds—even those with the lowest expense ratios—have management fees of almost 2 percent per year, an index fund can be run for less than a third of that amount. Indexing represents a sensible strategy that can enable nonprofessionals to obtain the advantages of emerging-markets investing with a simple one-stop-shopping approach.

The Case for Indexing

The controversy surrounding the concept of an emerging-market index fund is similar to the outrage that greeted the publication twenty-four years ago of the first edition of *A Random Walk Down Wall Street*. Index mutual funds did not exist in 1973, and Burton Malkiel caused a considerable stir by presenting the case for buying and holding a representative index of all stocks in the U.S. market (the global economy was just beginning to make its presence felt) and called for the establishment of index funds to be sold to the general public. Malkiel's argument then and now rests on the view that the U.S. capital markets are extremely efficient. When news arises about an individual stock or the stock market as a whole, professional investors act on this information and prices adjust without delay. If stock prices thus reflect all that is known at any point in time, even uninformed investors buying at current prices can do as well as professionals. As Malkiel put it in 1973, "a blindfolded chimpanzee throwing darts at *The Wall Street Journal* could do as well as the experts."

Moreover, by eschewing trading and active management, an index fund can be run at an extremely low expense rate and can thus minimize trading costs as well as taxes. Because stock markets tend to have a long-run uptrend with the growth of economic activity, sales of securities will usually involve realizing capital gains, which in countries such as the United States are taxed by both the federal government and most state governments. Buying and holding minimizes the realization of gains and thus maximizes after-tax returns.

The twenty-four years since *Random Walk* was first written have been extremely kind to the indexing thesis. Approximately 70 percent of actively managed mutual funds have regularly been outperformed by the broad stock market indexes in the United States. Index funds have produced net returns for individual investors that have been about 2 percentage points greater before tax than the average high-cost mutual fund. The differential after considering capital gains taxes is even greater. Moreover, while a few funds have managed to beat the index over long periods of time, the number of substantial outperformers can be counted on the fingers of both hands. And there is no way of knowing in advance who these investment stars will be. Past performance has proved to be a very unreliable guide to future profitability. Small wonder that indexing has now captured more than 25 percent of corporate pension fund money in the United States and has become an increasingly popular investment alternative. The Vanguard 500 Stock Index Fund is now the second largest equity mutual fund in the United States.

Malkiel and other indexing advocates won their argument because the growth of information technology has made the U.S. market enormously efficient. The world economy is another matter. Two central questions need to be addressed in the debate about creating global index funds that are similar in philosophy to those existing for the U.S. market: First, what constitutes a representative index of world stocks? And second, is the global market as efficient as the U.S. market?

Constructing an Index: Some Important Issues

As this book goes to press, there are only a handful of indexes claiming to represent stocks in developing countries. One of the most closely watched is the Morgan Stanley Capital International-Select Emerging Markets Index (MSCI), which is used as the model for the Vanguard Emerging Markets Index Fund, the only emerging-markets index fund available to the general public as of the start of 1997. MSCI covers twenty-six countries spread across

Africa, Asia, Europe, and Latin America. The stocks in the index are ones in which foreigners are free to invest. Vanguard uses that index as a basis but subtracts some countries where it is difficult to invest (or where certain restrictions, such as redemption restrictions, apply) and adds two countries, Hong Kong and Singapore. Figure 8-1 presents the composition of the Vanguard index as of the end of 1996. The weights in the fund are determined by the market capitalization of the individual stocks. By market capitalization, we mean simply the number of shares outstanding multiplied by the price per share.[1]

FIGURE 8-1

**GDP Versus Vanguard Emerging
Markets Index Fund Weights**

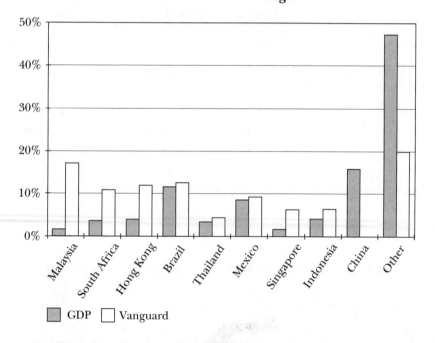

The Vanguard index is admittedly not perfect. First, the weight of each country in the portfolio is determined by the total market value of all the investable stocks of that country. Thus, the larger

1. Vanguard does impose maximum country weights on its index portfolio.

the country's stock market, the more money will be invested in that country. As a result, many countries with underdeveloped stock markets, whose stocks are not freely available for investment, are likely to be underrepresented despite their huge economies. For instance, China is the largest emerging market in terms of its total output of goods and services, or gross domestic product (GDP); yet in 1996 it had a weight of only 0.5 percent in the MSCI. Of course, investors obtain some exposure to China from the Hong Kong companies in the index and Hong Kong became part of China in July 1997. As can be seen in Figure 8-1, the country that has the most weight is Malaysia, despite the fact that China's economy is many times the size of that country's.

Second, since a value-weighted index is based on market prices, it tends to increase the weight of countries whose stocks have recently done well. As a result, it may lead investors to increase their exposure to markets where prices may be under the influence of some kind of speculative tulip bulb craze. A recent example of the experience of index investors in developed international markets will clarify the point.

As mentioned in Chapter Six, the major index of developed overseas stocks is also published by Morgan Stanley and is popularly known as the EAFE Index. The weights in the index are based on the market weights of all the available stocks in each market. During the late 1980s, the Japanese stock market experienced an extraordinary rise that was widely interpreted as a speculative bubble. The stock market doubled and then doubled again with P/E ratios approaching 100, far in excess of anything experienced in Japan's financial history. As the prices of Japanese stocks rose, so did the weight of Japan's market as a percentage of the EAFE Index total. Investors who bought the EAFE Index found that almost two-thirds of their portfolios were invested in overpriced Japanese stocks. Had the index been weighted according to the relative sizes of the constituent countries' economies (as measured by their total GDP), Japanese stocks would have been limited to about one-third of the index. Thus, investing in an index that is market value weighted will not protect an investor from being overinvested in precisely those stock markets experiencing a speculative mania. During the 1990s, the Japanese stock market crashed, losing almost two-thirds of its value at its low point.

Evaluating the Efficiency of Emerging Markets

Even analysts who accept the case for indexing in a market such as the United States would argue vigorously against extending the concept to international markets. Emerging markets in particular are by their nature inefficient. A no-brain index could never outwit a professional investor on treacherous overseas bourses, or so it is said. Emerging markets are small, obscure investment arenas that are not carefully followed by professionals. Information is of poor quality and hard to come by. Perhaps in the United States, it is argued, there are few hidden nuggets of value to uncover. But surely in less efficient emerging markets, good professional managers should be able to find exceptional bargains. The best values may not even be included in the indexes used to track emerging economies. Thus, indexing might be a very bad idea for international markets in general and especially for emerging markets.

It may well be true that stocks in emerging markets are less efficiently priced than in developed markets. But we believe that indexing still has much to recommend it as a serviceable way of diversifying one's portfolio. The transactions costs of trading stocks on emerging markets are so large that they are likely to offset any advantage an active manager might gain. Emerging markets are very illiquid; that is, there are few active buyers or sellers of individual stocks available at any time. Thus, in emerging markets the bid–asked spread—the difference between the price a dealer is willing to pay a seller and the price at which the dealer will fill a buyer's order—tends to be several times the spread existing in a market such as the New York Stock Exchange.

Moreover, if a fund manager wishes to sell a large block of a particular stock, the dealer's bid price is likely to fall precipitously.

This is the "roach motel" theory of emerging markets. According to a popular U.S. television commercial advertising a trap to kill cockroaches, "The roaches can check in—but they can't check out." Similarly, it is usually impossible to unload large stock positions in emerging markets at current market prices. No manager can move large chunks of money from stock to stock or from one emerging market to another without incurring substantial costs. To be successful in emerging markets, one must be a long-term holder. This severely limits the potential gains from active management.

John Bogle, the chairman of The Vanguard Group—the mutual fund complex that pioneered indexing—has estimated that the indexing advantage in transactions costs minimization is particularly large in international markets. Adding management expenses and transactions costs, the expense of running a public index fund of large-capitalization U.S. securities for small investors is about 0.2 percent, while actively managed U.S. large-capitalization equity funds entail total expenses (including transactions costs) of about 1.6 percent per year. The index advantage is thus approximately 1.4 percent (called "140 basis points" by professionals—a basis point is one one-hundredth of 1 percent). Bogle's estimates for international funds are shown in Table 8-1.

TABLE 8-1
Index Advantage for International Funds (in basis points)

	Index Funds	*Actively Managed Funds*
Expense ratio	35	175
Transactions costs	8	248
Total	43	423
index advantage = 380 basis points (3.8 percentage points)		

SOURCE: John Bogle, "Six Things to Remember About Indexing," address to Association for Investment Management and Research Conference, Atlanta, Georgia, May 8, 1996.

Indexing thus saves almost 4 percentage points per year, not including the tax savings. The above figures were estimated for international funds in general. However, expenses and transactions costs in emerging markets are even higher than in developed international markets, suggesting that the savings in those markets are even greater than Bogle's estimates. In addition, investors in some emerging markets must grapple with a variety of taxes on securities trading as well as with less liquidity and other restrictions. Thus, while emerging markets may be quite inefficient, the costs of professional management make it difficult to exploit any such inefficiencies or even the predictable patterns described in Chapter Two. The bottom line is that even superior managers are unlikely to offset these substantial costs.

Indexing Wins Again

Despite the admitted imperfections of current emerging-market indexes, the evidence still suggests that they outdistance active managers and are therefore the better buy. The MSCI, for example, returned 13.81 percent per year from 1991 through the end of 1995, while the average actively managed emerging-markets equity fund returned only 11.68 percent annually. (Both returns were calculated based on both dividends and capital gains.) During that period, the MSCI beat every other emerging-market fund that had a continuous five-year record. Figure 8-2 presents the percentage of managed emerging-market funds that were outperformed by the MSCI in different periods from 1991 through 1996. What is interesting is that even though there were subperiods when some managed funds outperformed the index, when one looks at the results over different five-year periods, the index fund beat 100 percent of the actively managed funds.

If we move from emerging-market investing to global investing in general, the evidence continues to put the odds in favor of indexing. The investment firm of Daniels and Alldredge publishes a global stock index called the Quantidex Index, which includes se-

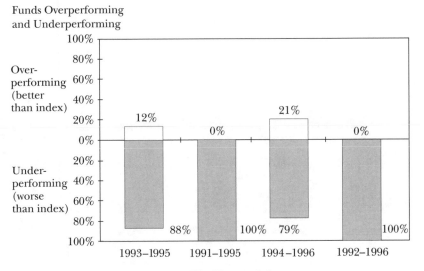

FIGURE 8-2

Percentage of Actively Managed Emerging-Market Funds Underperforming the MSCI Emerging-Markets Index

SOURCES: Lipper Analytical Services; The Vanguard Group.

curities from all developed and developing nations. It compares the performance of its index to the results of almost five hundred actively managed equity mutual funds that invest in U.S. stocks, multinational corporations, and securities of foreign countries, including emerging markets. The results for 1987–1996 are shown in Figure 8-3. The figure shows the number of funds that did worse than the index and the number that did better. The vast majority of the funds (about 90 percent) failed to match the index, many by a substantial amount. Only a handful of funds beat the index by a significant amount.

Active managers argue that they can select the best countries in which to invest and avoid those that are likely to get into trouble. After the fact, there will always be professional investment managers who will proclaim that they predicted a crisis such as the Mexican currency debacle of the mid-1990s. Active managers claim that they are able to protect their investors from the inevitable disasters that make particular emerging markets sub-

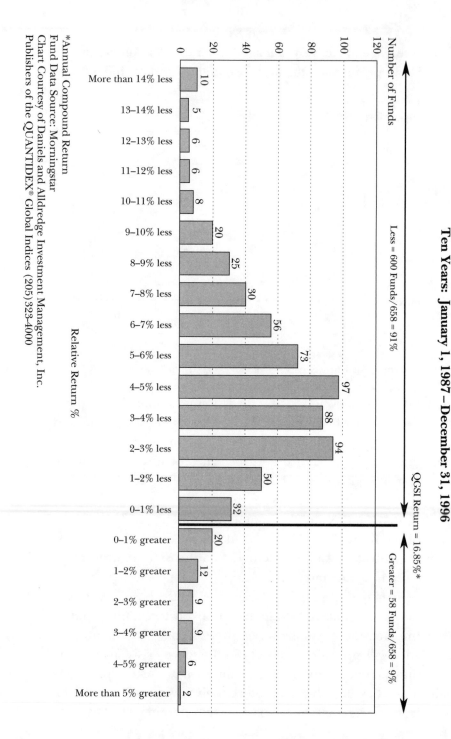

FIGURE 8-3

Quantidex Global Stock Index Versus 658 Stock Mutual Funds,
Ten Years: January 1, 1987 – December 31, 1996

*Annual Compound Return
Fund Data Source: Morningstar
Chart Courtesy of Daniels and Alldredge Investment Management, Inc.
Publishers of the QUANTIDEX® Global Indices (205)323-4000

merge temporarily. But most crises that befall these markets are imperfectly predictable, and few active managers are able to forecast them in advance. The statistics of actual performance demonstrate that it is simply not feasible to make large shifts among markets in advance of the volatile price movements that accompany unfavorable events.

The index investor relies on the statistics of chance just as the owner of a gambling casino does. The casino operator knows that on any particular evening some of his blackjack tables will lose money to a few lucky gamblers. Indeed, it is possible that the whole casino will lose money for an entire day. But a diversified portfolio of tables, especially over time, is likely to provide handsome returns since the odds are well in favor of the house. Emerging markets have some characteristics of a gambling casino, and fortunately, over time, the odds are stacked in favor of the investor. With growth in the emerging economies, investments in general are likely to provide generous returns. The index investor may be unsure which countries will, in fact, turn out to offer the best returns and which countries will disappoint. But the indexer is certain to have some representation of both the best and the worst economies and, on average, is guaranteed to enjoy whatever growth materializes in the developing world well into the new millennium.

While it is true that over certain periods of time some active international managers do beat the indexes, there seems to be no way to tell in advance just who those managers will be. Past performance is not a reliable guide—you cannot assure yourself of finding a manager with superior skill simply by picking funds with above-average past records. For example, studies we have performed show that the most successful managers from one period of time do not outperform the others in subsequent periods. The most successful investment managers of the 1980s have not been superior during the 1990s. Nobel Laureate Paul Samuelson sums up the difficulty in the following parable: Suppose it were demonstrated that one out of twenty alcoholics could learn to become a moderate social drinker. The experienced clinician would answer,

"Even if it is true, act as if it were false, for you will never identify that one in twenty." Moreover, in the attempt, nineteen people could revert to alcoholism. Samuelson concludes that investors should forsake the search for tiny needles in such huge haystacks.

Thus the gains of one investment manager and another balance out, and the transactions costs incurred by the managers detract from their performance. The other big detractor from performance is fund expenses, which average about 2 percent per year for actively managed emerging market funds versus less than 0.6 point for the largest public index fund. Like greyhounds at the dog track, professional emerging-market equity managers do not appear to be capable of winning their race with the mechanical rabbit.

Some critics of indexing argue that the strategy is one of "guaranteed mediocrity." But experience conclusively shows that index fund buyers are likely to obtain results exceeding those of the typical fund manager, whose large advisory fees and substantial portfolio turnover tend to reduce investment returns. The fact is that index performance is superior performance.

Available Index Instruments

How, then, can an investor pursue an indexing strategy? The obvious answer is to purchase a mutual fund that simply buys and holds all the stocks of a broad-based emerging-markets index. As this book goes to press, there is only one emerging-markets index fund available to the public: the Vanguard Emerging Markets Index Fund.

The Vanguard Emerging Markets Index Fund[2]

As mentioned earlier, the Vanguard fund seeks to match the performance of the Morgan Stanley Capital International-Select

2. The reader should be aware that Burton Malkiel is a director of The Vanguard Group of Investment Companies.

Emerging Markets Index (MSCI) plus the markets of Hong Kong and Singapore. It invests in some 525 stocks in countries spread across four continents.

The Vanguard fund tries to match the market's results, not outperform it. To do this, the fund holds the same stocks as those included in the index, or at least a representative sample. The fund is no-load in the sense that there is no sales fee, but Vanguard does impose a 1.5 percent transactions fee on the amount of new fund purchases. This fee, which is paid to the portfolio rather than to Vanguard, is imposed to cover the large commission and trading costs incurred when the fund invests the funds received from investors. The fee is waived if dividends and capital gains distributions are used to reinvest in the fund.

The fund also imposes a 1 percent redemption fee, again paid to the fund itself rather than to the Vanguard company. The purpose of these fees is to allocate the transactions costs of purchases and sales to the individuals causing these transactions to take place. Without such fees, the transactions costs would be allocated to all investors in the fund, thereby reducing performance. Because buyers and sellers both bear these costs, the portfolio is better able to track the index closely. These fees are designed to make the portfolio unattractive to speculators and making it attractive only to "buy-and-hold" investors who are willing to make a long-term allocation of part of their assets to these markets.

Since it is based on the MSCI Index, the Vanguard fund also includes the weaknesses of that index. As mentioned above, some major countries, such as China, are underrepresented in the index, and if any market becomes subject to a speculative bubble, it will be overrepresented in the fund.

To correct for these problems, we suggest that investors pursue a strategy of indexing with modification. The basic idea is to add those countries that are underrepresented in the index portfolio by adding closed-end country funds. For example, the underweighting of China in the MSCI Index could be corrected by purchasing the Templeton Dragon Fund or the Templeton China World Fund at a discount. Investors can use the alternative set of weights based upon the relative GDPs of the constituent economies in Figure 8-1 to check for overweighting if it gets to be tulip time in a specific market. By adding funds to the Vanguard Index Fund, the overweighting of certain markets can thus be slightly reduced.

We realize that it is not possible to compensate completely for an index fund's overweighting of some markets. Moreover, in some markets the composition of the index may be overweighted with certain industries. For example, real estate companies represent well over one-half of the Hong Kong stock market index. Nonetheless, we are convinced that an index fund investor, especially if he augments his fund with investments in underrepresented areas, is likely to benefit fully from the attractive returns we feel emerging markets will yield into the twenty-first century.

Other Index Products: World Equity Benchmark Securities (WEBS)

Other index products have come onto the scene during the late 1990s. These are called World Equity Benchmark Securities (WEBS). As of the beginning of 1997, there were seventeen WEBS, designed to track the Morgan Stanley Capital indices for seventeen countries. While most WEBS cover developed-country indexes, the WEBS of particular interest to emerging-market investors are those that track the indexes of Hong Kong, Mexico, and Singapore securities. These securities, developed by the investment firm of Morgan Stanley, are listed on the American Stock Exchange.

WEBS combine the best features of both open-end and closed-end funds. They are open-end investment companies, but unlike open-end funds distributed by mutual fund companies, they trade on a stock exchange. However, WEBS eliminate a major potential problem of closed-end funds, which, as we have indicated, can trade at a discount or premium to NAV, depending in part on investor sentiment toward the market in which the fund is investing.

WEBS are designed to eliminate premiums and discounts via an open-end structure that should make them unsustainable. Unlike closed-end funds, WEBS can be redeemed in kind by investors. Suppose, for example, that a WEBS was trading at a substantial discount from its NAV. An investor could redeem a portion of the entire portfolio of the WEBS and receive shares in the constituent companies. The investor could then sell these shares on the open market and gain an arbitrage profit less the transactions costs associated with the redemption process. This potential arbitrage mechanism is designed to prevent the occurrence of significant discounts on the WEBS shares.

A similar arbitrage mechanism prevents WEBS from selling at a premium. Additional WEBS can be "created" by having an investor buy a portfolio of constituent shares, deposit them with the WEBS manager, and receive WEBS shares. A premium should not persist because arbitragers could continuously create more WEBS units, which could then be sold on the open market at a premium. In fact, these potential arbitrage mechanisms appear to have worked well in that WEBS have, in fact, been trading essentially at NAV.

Like index funds, WEBS are invested passively and are designed to replicate the indices they track. Because their management is passive, their fees and expenses have generally been something less than 1 percent of asset value per year, compared with an average expense ratio of almost 2 percent for closed-end fund shares. Unfortunately, as this book goes to press, WEBS are available only for a handful of emerging markets and thus do not yet permit an investor to replicate a broad emerging-market index. Moreover, while the expense ratios for WEBS are low compared with other closed-end and open-end funds, they are somewhat higher than those of the Vanguard index fund. On the other hand, if an investor wanted to take a position in the Hong Kong market, for example, and preferred to do it with a low-cost index fund rather than through a managed open- or closed-end investment company, the Hong Kong WEBS would be a quite serviceable and low-cost way of obtaining that exposure. Particularly if closed-end funds are not available at larger-than-average discounts, these index products can be excellent diversifiers.

It should be noted that WEBS trade in dollars while the underlying shares trade in local currency. The managers of WEBS make no attempt to hedge currency values, so investors should be aware that they are exposed to currency fluctuations despite the fact that the instruments trade in dollars.

CHAPTER NINE

The Self-Directed Approach: Actively Managing Your Emerging-Market Portfolio

THIS CHAPTER IS a contradiction, a "logical incongruity" as Webster's dictionary would have it, because it goes against our advice. In the previous chapter, we advised you to use a passive index approach or buy closed-end funds when they are available at substantial discounts. Here we give you guidelines on how you alone can seek riches among the treacherous shoals of emerging markets. We have written this material for those who regard emerging-market investing as a challenge and an exciting game that is too much fun to hand over to the direction of someone else. It is also written for those who must truly be unique individuals—investment geniuses who possess the capability to consistently beat all other people and institutions in the search for financial success.

The nineteenth-century English essayist Sydney Smith once wrote that contradiction set him to sneezing. It sets us to issuing one final warning: We do not believe you can consistently beat a simple buy-and-hold indexing strategy. This belief is so important that we review it once again.

Pitfalls of the Self-Directed Approach

Investors who choose to manage their emerging-market portfolios actively usually do so on the premise that emerging markets are filled with hidden opportunities; that, in other words, they are inefficient. This inefficiency is due to excessive local government regulation, antiquated trading systems, and a lack of investment experience among local investors. With access to fast computers and comprehensive databases, so the thinking goes, individuals can use technological superiority to obtain superior risk-adjusted returns.

Thus, if anyone could exploit inefficiencies, it would have to be professional investors, those with access to expensive computers and databases. Not only that, but many of these people, such as Mark Mobius, also have large travel budgets and personally inspect emerging-market corporate managements and their products. These investment professionals say that by selecting the best individual issues directly and by overweighting particular emerging markets in their portfolios, they can find the best values and easily beat a dull index.

Our thesis, repeated once again, is that most pros cannot exploit inefficiencies and consistently build a winning portfolio of individual emerging-market equities. In other words, as far as stock selection goes, market efficiency has beaten the pros in the overseas rush. And if the pros cannot win, neither can you.

Let us start by reviewing the question of whether emerging markets are really inefficient. Economists often use two measures to examine stock market efficiency: information efficiency and economic efficiency. Information efficiency holds that stock prices always reflect all available information. It implies that past information, such as the history of stock prices, corporate earnings, and general economic statistics and projections, will not help predict future stock prices. Economic efficiency holds that no investor can consistently obtain excess risk-adjusted returns. It implies that an uninformed investor buying at existing market prices can do as well as an expert, provided that both investors' portfolios have the same degree of risk.

There is some evidence that emerging markets may not be informationally efficient; in other words, they may be somewhat predictable. In a study published in 1992, Campbell Harvey, a Duke

University economist, found that price changes from month to month for many emerging markets are highly correlated, unlike the case in the United States. This suggests that prices do not react to news immediately and that future stock prices are somewhat predictable from past stock price changes. Harvey further discovered that U.S. interest rates have significant predictive power over the future returns of several emerging markets. In a 1996 report, however, Geert Bekaert, at Stanford University, and others found that emerging-market returns and risks tend to vary substantially over time. This suggests that while there is certainly some predictability based on past returns, realized returns may be too volatile to make the forecast useful or worth the trading costs associated with rebalancing the portfolio. To put it another way, there is so much noise accompanying signals that any predictable patterns are financially useless when burdened by the inevitable and substantial trading costs involved.

While there is some evidence suggesting that emerging markets may not be informationally efficient, there is little evidence suggesting that they are economically inefficient. As pointed out in the last chapter, professional emerging-market fund managers do not outperform the various emerging-market indexes that serve as investment benchmarks. This suggests that even professionals fail to exploit whatever market inefficiencies exist. Thus, our conclusion is that while emerging markets are not as efficient as developed markets, they are also not places where obvious unexploited arbitrage opportunities are lying around waiting to be snatched up by investors.

Why can't the high-tech, buy-and-sell fund managers outperform the low-tech buy-and-holders in emerging markets? We believe there are three basic reasons. First, despite their backward technology, emerging markets are reasonably efficient, and their prices reflect the savvy of local investors and their better understanding of local politics. Thus, as much as possible, emerging-market stock prices already incorporate expected political events, which have proven to be some of the most important factors in determining stock market returns. Second, the huge transactions costs and market volatility in emerging markets may have prevented fund managers from taking advantage of any noticeable inefficiencies. Third, fund managers are competing not only with the locals but also with their high-tech Western peers, who have recently shown increased interest in emerging stock markets. As a result of this competition, emerging stock markets come reasonably close to a condition of economic efficiency.

Gearing Up

You may still be convinced that you can disprove our thesis, or at least that the search itself is too much fun to pass up. But before you set out to outperform an emerging-market index, you need to have access to good investment information. You will find a lot of information at public libraries or local bookstores. You should read the financial and international pages of *The New York Times* and *The Wall Street Journal.* International publications, such as the *Financial Times, The Economist,* and *Far Eastern Economic Review,* should also be on your "must-read" list. Major investment advisory services may also provide some useful information. The country reports by The Economist Intelligence Unit provide excellent country analyses. Business magazines, such as *Business Week, Forbes,* and *Fortune,* may also be useful for gaining exposure to investment ideas. Finally, the Internet can be a useful source of financial news regarding emerging markets. Table 9-1 shows some useful Web sites for emerging-market investors.

Table 9-1

Useful Web Sites for Emerging-Market Information

Financial news:

Bloomberg Business News: www.bloomberg.com/bbn/index.html

Financial Times (free, but registration required): www.ft.com

The Wall Street Journal (by paid subscription only): www.wsj.com

The New York Times: www.nytimes.com

Links to newspapers around the world (includes many emerging-market sources): www.cs.vu.nl/~gerben/news.html

Data sources:

Links to governments' statistical servers: www.isds.duke.edu/sites/gov.html

World Factbook (good source of general data on every country in the world) www.odci.gov/cia/publications/95fact/index.html

General emerging market sites:

IFC's Emerging Market Database (tracks daily and weekly performance of emerging-market stock indexes): www.ifc.org/EMDB/EMDBHOME.htm

BradyNet (everything you ever wanted to know about Brady bonds, including current prices): www.bradynet.com

Chicago Mercantile Exchange (emerging-market pages targeted mostly at investors in futures and options): www.cme.com/market/emerging/index.html

Region- and country-specific sites:

(*Note:* Those listed here are only a few examples of the many sites relevant to emerging markets that can be found by searching, or surfing, the World Wide Web.)

Africa News on the World Wide Web: www.nando.net/ans/

ChinaInvest (links related to China, Taiwan, and Hong Kong): www.globalvillager.com/villager/CIDir

The Indian Economy Overview: www.m-web.com

LatinWorld (links about all Latin American countries): www.latinworld.com

Maximov (Russia): www.maximov.com

Lists of links:

Financial Data Finder: www.cob.ohio-state.edu/dept/fin/osudata.htm

Links to international stock exchanges (must be registered with *Financial Times* to access): www.ft.com/hippocampus/c18e.htm

SOURCE: Compiled by Sari Carp.

Since information on emerging-market companies is somewhat hard to find and difficult to comprehend, it may be helpful to use a full-service broker. In determining which broker to use, the most important criterion is whether the firm can furnish quality information. The questions to ask include: Does the firm have a large and well-respected international research department? Does it have overseas representatives producing extensive on-site research rather than home-office analysts doing secondhand news summaries? Does it have a relatively long history of doing business and managing funds in emerging markets? Again, we warn that there is little evidence that the use of any full-service broker can ensure that you will do any better than professional fund managers. Nevertheless, you will need to be at least as well informed as your competitors, if not more so.

Seven Investment Tips

The following tips will help you manage your emerging-market portfolio more profitably. There is, however, an important caveat: While we believe these tips may help improve your returns in the short run, we also feel that their effectiveness will diminish over time as more investors utilize them. Indeed, they may already be less effective than they were in the early 1990s.

Tip 1: Look at Regions, Not Companies

Individual investors interested in active portfolio management should concentrate on country rather than individual stock selection. We base this tip on the following observations. First, the transactions costs of buying individual stocks are so high that they can wipe out much of your potential gain. Second, emerging-market stocks are highly illiquid, and you will often find you cannot sell them when you want to. Third, many studies have found that most emerging-market stocks are highly correlated with their domestic-market index. Thus, investors can probably achieve most of their investment returns by investing in the right market rather than trying to pick the best companies. Fourth, closed-end country funds, or WEBS, are fairly liquid and tend to be better diversified than a portfolio of a few stocks is. Buying these instruments allows you to reduce transactions costs and investment risk. Fifth, after finding a particularly attractive emerging market with high growth potential, you may be able to buy its closed-end fund at a deep discount, thus getting a double bargain. As indicated in Chapter Seven, closed-end country funds often sell at substantial discounts from the market value of the securities held in the fund's portfolio.

If, however, you remain committed to investing directly in emerging-market shares, there are two ways to do so. The first is to purchase shares of emerging-market companies in the local markets on which they are traded. For most investors this is not practical because of the high transactions costs associated with foreign exchange conversion, account custody, and dividend collection. The second method is to buy emerging-market shares traded in the United States. These are sold in the form of American Depository Receipts (ADRs), which represent ownership of foreign shares traded in the United States. Emerging-market companies issue these dollar-denominated, easily accessible shares in order to attract U.S. investors. As shown in Table 9-2, at the end of 1995 there were 663 ADRs traded in the United States, with a total market capitalization of more than $672 billion.

One obvious advantage of investing through ADRs is that you avoid the costs and difficulties of trading directly in overseas markets. All trades are settled in U.S. dollars, which obviates the need to convert dollars into foreign currencies and vice versa. Another advantage is that the listing requirements of the U.S. securities exchanges demand a higher level of conformity to American accounting and reporting practices, which makes it easier for investors to perform various valuation analyses. One major drawback is that many ADRs are illiquid. Even the relatively liquid stocks often carry a bid–asked spread of 50 cents, much higher than the typical 12.5 cents for most U.S. stocks. Another problem is that some ADRs are not listed on exchanges but are traded on the over-the-counter market, where reporting requirements are less stringent.

TABLE 9-2

Emerging-Market Companies That Issue American Depository Receipts (ADRs) and Their Market Capitalizations

	Number of ADRs	*Market Capitalization (in billions)*
Argentina	20	$26.7
Brazil	49	57.3
Chile	21	24.3
Colombia	13	2.2
Mexico	88	61.6
Peru	8	0.9
Venezuela	13	1.7
China	19	4.9
Hong Kong	94	202.0
Korea	22	51.6
Philippines	16	22.5
Taiwan	25	12.1
India	74	24.4
Indonesia	7	2.4
Malaysia	18	37.5
Pakistan	6	1.3
Singapore	16	NA
Sri Lanka	2	0.1
Thailand	8	18.0
Czech Republic	2	NA
Greece	4	1.2
Hungary	8	0.3
Poland	2	NA
Portugal	5	NA
South Africa	114	118.1
Turkey	8	NA
Zimbabwe	1	NA
Total	663	NA

SOURCE: Bank of New York, *The Complete Depository Receipt Directory*, 1995.

Tip 2: Use Price-Earnings Ratios and Dividend Yields to Find Investment Bargains

To check out a market's past and present financial outlook, focus on two key measurements: the dividend yield and the P/E ratio for the market as a whole. These indicators help you gauge whether a particular market is reasonably priced, based on the country's growth potential. (The dividend yield for a stock is calculated by dividing the stated annual dividend by the company's stock price; the P/E ratio is obtained by dividing the price by the company's earnings per share. The dividend yield or P/E ratio for a market refers to the average for a representative index of the major companies in the particular country.)

Despite the fact that accounting standards may differ from those of Western countries, we believe that a comparison of a market's current dividend yield and P/E ratio to their historical levels still provides a useful guide for the valuation of the market. While skeptics may argue that you can never tell whether an emerging market is undervalued, we do feel that you can roughly gauge when a stock market seems to be reasonably priced, and you can certainly get a warning as to when a market has risen to unsustainable heights. We suggest that unless there is a reason to believe that a country's future growth prospects have improved dramatically, you should choose countries for investment whose stocks are selling at multiples below, or not very much above, their historical levels.

Can dividend yields and P/E ratios help forecast long-term stock market returns? We presented some evidence on the usefulness of P/E ratios in Chapter Two, where we mentioned that future returns for various emerging markets tended to be large when stocks could be purchased at relatively low P/E ratios. Additional evidence shown in Figures 9-1 and 9-2 from the experience of the Hong Kong market supports this conclusion. These charts present the initial dividend yield and the P/E ratio at which Hong Kong stocks could be purchased in different time periods and the ten-year future returns realized from those valuation levels.

Figure 9-1 was constructed by measuring the market's dividend yield at the start of each quarter, beginning in 1974. The observations were then divided into five equal groups, according to the levels of dividend yields for the quarters. The first group contains the periods when stocks were offering very high yields, above 6 percent. The next three groups include the periods when Hong Kong stocks had slightly lower yields. The last group measures periods when stocks sold at yields of less than 3 percent—that is, the periods when stocks were much more richly valued.

Figure 9-2 is a similar chart that divides the same quarters into five different groups, depending on the P/E ratio at the start of the period. The bars in each chart show the following ten-year

FIGURE 9-1

Average Ten-Year Returns When Hong Kong Stocks Were Purchased at Different Dividend Yields

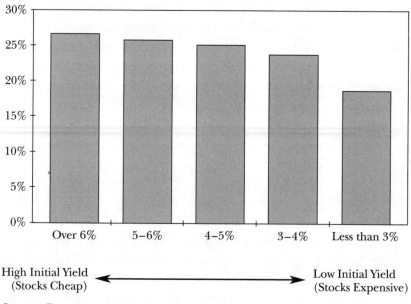

SOURCE: Datastream; authors' computations.

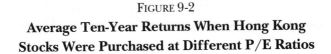

FIGURE 9-2

**Average Ten-Year Returns When Hong Kong
Stocks Were Purchased at Different P/E Ratios**

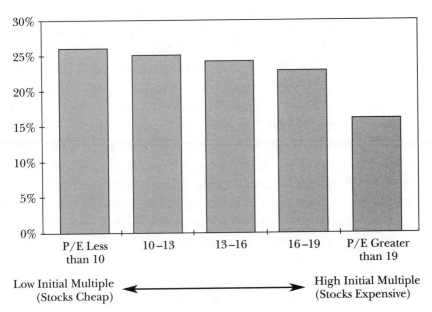

SOURCE: Datastream; authors' computations.

rate of return from the different initial valuation levels. The result
is quite clear. While on average investors have earned about 23
percent per year from the Hong Kong market since 1974, rates of
return were above average when Hong Kong stocks were bought
at relatively high yields and low P/E ratios and tended to be lower
than average if stocks were bought at relatively low yields and high
P/Es.

Based on this analysis, a sensible way of gauging the valuation
levels of various markets is to obtain from your broker or financial
service the yields and P/E ratios for various emerging-market indexes and compare them to their historical levels. If there is little
change in earnings growth prospects, you should consider it a

warning signal when stocks are selling well above their historical multiples.

This rule can also be used to compare valuation levels between markets. If two countries appear to have identical growth prospects, the country whose stocks sell at higher dividend yields and lower P/E ratios can be said to offer the best value. As we mentioned in Chapter One, the rule devised by Peter Lynch should be particularly useful in comparing markets. The Lynch ratio divided the long-term growth rate for a stock by its P/E ratio (or the P/E average for the stock market as a whole). If, for example, a stock had a projected annual growth rate of 10 percent and a P/E ratio of 20, the Lynch ratio would be 0.5. The higher the Lynch ratio, the more attractive the market. The Lynch ratio implies that it is all right to pay a higher P/E ratio for a stock as long as its growth prospects are commensurately higher. What is ideal, of course, is to find markets with high growth prospects and moderate P/E ratios.

Be particularly wary of stocks and markets with very high P/E ratios and many years of growth already discounted in the prices. If earnings disappoint and actually decline, you will be hit with a double loss: the multiple will drop along with the earnings and heavy losses will result. This warning can help you avoid bubble markets, such as the Taiwanese market in the early 1990s when the market P/E ratio soared far above historical averages. It can also help you avoid bubble stocks, such as Mazda Industry and Leasing Company of India and Happy Flying of Shanghai, which were caught up in the speculative frenzies described in Chapter Five. On the other hand, when P/E ratios are low and good growth is actually realized, stock prices are likely to rise both because earnings have grown and because P/E ratios may rise as well.

There is some evidence that overweighting markets with low P/E ratios can lead to larger future returns. Figure 9-3 presents an analysis of returns for emerging markets with different initial P/E ratios. The figure shows that the best returns over the 1988–1996 period tended to come from those emerging markets where the

P/E ratios were low at the beginning of the period. Of course, it is important to realize that the transactions costs of adjusting one's portfolio to overweight low-P/E-ratio markets are not considered in the calculation. Considerable additional switching would also be required to be invested each year only in those markets with the lowest P/E ratios. Moreover, an investor who confined his emerging-market holdings to markets with the lowest P/E ratios would be holding a very risky and undiversified portfolio. Finally, it is not certain that such valuation techniques will continue to work as well in the future. Nevertheless, the data do support a strategy of overweighting markets with low P/E ratios.

FIGURE 9-3

Emerging-Market Returns Versus P/E Ratios

Returns: Dec. 1989 – July 1996
(Percent Per Annum)

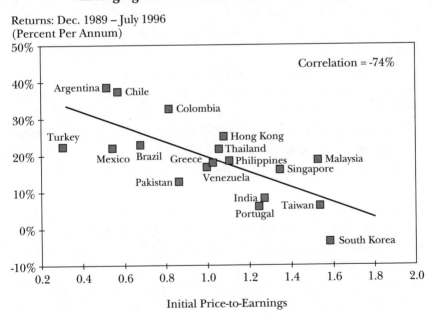

Initial Price-to-Earnings

Historically, future returns have been higher when various emerging-market indexes could be purchased at low P/E ratios (P/E ratio, December 1988, versus 1989–1996 returns).

SOURCE: Smith Barney & Company.

Tip 3: Overweight Markets with Low Price-to-Book-Value Ratios

The price-to-book-value (P/BV) ratio is another useful measure of the attractiveness of stocks or markets. This measure is computed by dividing the market price of each stock by its book value per share (the stated value of the company's assets divided by the number of shares outstanding). A low P/BV ratio (less than 1) implies that you can buy the company for less than the value of the assets on the books. As mentioned in Chapter Two, studies have found that P/BV ratios have been useful in explaining emerging-market equity returns (see Figure 2-3). Markets with low P/BV ratios have outperformed those with high ratios. This may seem surprising, given the substantial accounting differences that exist across emerging markets in the world. Empirical research, however, suggests that the accounting differences have not diminished the usefulness of this ratio.

Numerous studies have also confirmed that the same results hold among stocks listed on the New York Stock Exchange despite the fact that accounting differences often exist across industrial sectors in the United States. The question here is not whether P/BV ratios are accurate measures of valuation relationships across emerging markets but whether the ratios can help us forecast future returns across different markets. The answer appears to be "yes." Using historical data, researchers at Smith Barney have suggested, as can be seen in Figure 9-4, that, by forming a portfolio that overweights low-P/BV-ratio markets and underweights high-P/BV-ratio markets, an investor can significantly outperform the market capitalization weighted index, at least before transactions costs. Again, however, one should be cautious in assuming that such outperformance will continue in the future.

Tip 4: Watch Out for False Bargains

Low P/E or P/BV ratios could be the result of poor growth prospects or high risks rather than unexploited market inefficiencies. In China and Indonesia, for example, many low-P/E-ratio

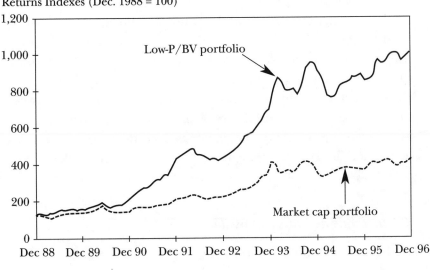

FIGURE 9-4

Low-P/BV Portfolio Outperforms Market Capitalization Portfolio

Returns Indexes (Dec. 1988 = 100)

SOURCE: Smith Barney & Company.

and low-P/BV-ratio stocks occur in poorly managed enterprises partially owned by the state government. Moreover, the transactions costs involved in trying to exploit these relationships could wipe out any profits. Thus, investors need to supplement the above rules with other analyses of market valuations and risks. This will help balance bargain hunting with risk exposure. It is important to note that a portfolio consisting of only low-P/E-ratio or low-P/BV-ratio stocks from a single country, or an imperfectly diversified portfolio, could be extremely risky. Therefore, while you may decide to over- or underweight some markets, you should always maintain a reasonably well diversified portfolio.

Tip 5: Buy Stocks in Countries Where Political Risk Is Subsiding

Political risk is a major factor affecting emerging-market returns. Its reduction both improves the prospect of future cash flows for business firms and reduces the risk premium by which such cash flows are discounted. Thus, any reduction in political risk is likely to boost stock returns directly. This is why successful emerging-market investing demands political as well as economic savvy. The key to success here is sensing the wind of political change several months before such change actually occurs. Any increase in political stability is likely to reduce investors' risk perceptions about the country. Similarly, countries that are moving rapidly toward a free-market economy and whose income gains are widely distributed are likely to be viewed very favorably by world investors. This said, we recognize that many shocks (the death of a country's leader, a military coup, a weather disaster, etc.) are unlikely to be predictable.

Tip 6: Trade as Little as Possible

We have repeatedly warned about the extraordinarily high transactions costs of trading in emerging markets. A round-trip commission (on a purchase and sale) can be as high as 7 percent of the total transaction and represent a much larger percentage of your profit. Particularly if markets are even close to being efficient, the benefit of trading is suspect. It makes a great deal of sense to minimize trading when the bites from your broker and tax collector are both large and certain. We do not suggest that you never sell a stock or a country fund on which you have a gain. The circumstances that led you to buy a certain stock or fund may have changed. A successful country fund, for example, might become overpriced during a speculative bubble and thus substantially overweighted in your portfolio, as in Taiwan during the late 1980s and Shanghai in the early 1990s. In such a circumstance, some paring back of an overweighted position can reduce risk. But switching from security to security or fund to fund should be a rare event, not a regular occurrence. In general, if you decide to invest in emerging markets, you should plan to be a long-term holder. Emerging-market investments are the kind of security to buy in planning for retirement many years in the future—not for buying a Porsche convertible as a Christmas present for a spouse.

Remember that the above tip applies to individual stock selection as well. To fans of individual stock selection, we suggest a two-step approach. First, use the above valuation rules (Tips 2 and 3) to help select attractive growth stocks. Here the trick is to find growth stocks that have not already been recognized by the market, which means that they are not selling at high P/E ratios. Cast your net wide, since many prime growth companies can be found in sectors that in developed countries are considered quite mature. For example, one of the fastest-growing Chilean companies is Chilgener, an electric utility. It is also worth noting that, given the volatile business environment in emerging markets, companies that can consistently produce earnings growth amid political turmoil deserve a particularly careful look.

Moreover, special attention should be given to local blue-chip companies. They tend to have important connections that may give investors some protection against corruption and extortion. It is also a plus if the company's managers own a substantial equity stake: in a free-market economy, self-interest is the most powerful incentive. Owning a large chunk of the company's stock tends to give the managers a good incentive to perform and play by the rules. We also suggest you underweight or avoid countries where corruption is so rampant that it begins to threaten economic growth and political stability.

After you have selected attractive stocks, use the above rules to select the "bargain" (high-growth, low-valuation, and declining-political-risk) countries and then overweight your holdings in those bargain countries. Here the important thing is to strike a fine balance between bargain hunting and diversification. Because we are skeptical about the ability of even professionals to add a great deal of value by placing huge bets on individual securities or individual countries, we believe the overriding goal should be wide diversification.

Tip 7: Prune Your Hedges Severely

There is currency risk whenever you invest outside your home country. For example, a U.S. investor who buys a Mexican security could lose money even when the stock goes up if the Mexican peso depreciates against the dollar. An example will illustrate the problem. In 1994, Teléfonos de México (Telmex), the major Mexican telephone company, sold at 11.50 Mexican pesos per share. By January 1997, Telmex had risen to 15 pesos per share. But in 1994, the exchange rate between Mexican pesos and U.S. dollars was 3.5 pesos to the dollar, while in January 1997, the exchange rate was almost 8 pesos to the dollar. Although Telmex had appreciated 30 percent in pesos, if a U.S. investor had to convert those pesos back into dollars, he would have found that the peso was worth less than half as much in dollars as was the case in 1994. Hence, the dollar price of a Telmex ADR (one ADR = 20 Mexican shares) on the New York Stock Exchange, where it is traded in the United States, actually fell from $67 per share to $37 per share, a 45 percent decline in price.

To guard against such a circumstance, some professional investors recommend that emerging-market investors always hedge the currency risk of a stock portfolio by taking offsetting positions in the currency markets. For example, a U.S. investor who converts dollars into pesos to buy Telmex might simultaneously sell pesos forward in the currency futures market, in effect converting the pesos back into dollars at a future time. Other professionals recommend selective hedging—taking offsetting currency futures positions only when a particular emerging-market currency is expected to depreciate. While we believe that there might be an appropriate role for hedging for bond investors, we do not recommend that stock investors attempt to do any hedging whatsoever, for the following reasons.

First, hedging can be expensive. Continuous hedging of Mexican pesos, for example, entails repeated transactions in the currency futures markets, and each transaction involves transactions charges as well as the posting of margin (security) deposits. Second, we are very skeptical about any investor's ability to implement a selective occasional hedging policy successfully. It is virtually impossible, even for professionals, to make correct calls on changes in currency values, and our reading of selective hedging is that it sometimes improves returns, sometimes reduces returns, and *always* involves substantial transactions costs, so that in the end it provides no net benefit. Finally, we believe that hedging may reduce the diversification benefits of emerging-market investing.

Recall that one of the strongest arguments for investing in emerging markets is that they can reduce the overall risk of a portfolio by improving diversification. As argued in Chapter Six, the gains from including different kinds of assets in a portfolio depend upon how closely the added assets are correlated with those already in the portfolio. Thus, an investor in the United States will find that adding some emerging-market stocks to a portfolio containing only U.S. stocks can reduce overall portfolio risk. The risk reduction is achieved because emerging-market stock returns are not highly correlated with U.S. stock returns. When emerging markets zig, U.S. stocks often zag, and an internationally diversified portfolio tends to produce more stable returns than one that includes only domestic-market securities. The key to risk reduction is to add types of assets and markets that are not highly correlated with the assets already in a portfolio.

This brings us to the heart of our objection to hedging. Not only is hedging expensive, it also does not lower the correlations between foreign and domestic equity returns. Indeed, in some instances, hedging increases the correlations among returns and thus tends to *reduce* the benefits of international diversification. We calculated the correlation coefficients between the returns of each emerging-market country and each emerging-market region with the returns from the U.S. stock market, and we found that most correlation coefficients for hedged emerging-market investments were either the same as the unhedged returns or, in some instances, even higher on a hedged basis. Thus, hedging does not improve the trade-off between risk and return. Indeed, in many instances it makes the trade-off *less* attractive. Consequently, since hedging involves both time and expense, we strongly recommend that investors do not attempt to control for currency risk. No additional benefits are likely to accrue to investors who attempt to reduce risk by hedging foreign currency equity returns.

Some Final Advice

We remain skeptical that anyone—even the pros—can, over the long run, beat the returns from an emerging-market index or from a diversified portfolio of closed-end funds selling at substantial discounts. If you still want to try, we think that country selection is preferable to individual stock selection. But even if you stick with country funds, we suggest you diversify broadly, because many geopolitical events that can move markets are largely unpredictable. For the intrepid few who wish to place their bets on just a few countries or regions or on individual emerging-market stocks, we think the tips in this chapter will tilt the odds of success a bit more in your favor. At the very least, they should make the hunt a little less dangerous.

CHAPTER TEN

Bargains in Bonds, Real Estate, and Natural Resources

IN A CELEBRATED exchange with Ernest Hemingway, F. Scott Fitzgerald is said to have remarked, "The rich are different from you and me." "Yes," replied Hemingway, "they have more money." And with more money comes the need for greater diversification to protect and enhance it. That's why it is important to look for investment opportunities that are available in assets other than stocks.

We believe that investors should first diversify their assets by including domestic government and corporate bonds as well as real estate in their overall portfolios. This is particularly true for those constructing a retirement plan. We also feel strongly that the equity or stock portion of that portfolio should include holdings in developed foreign as well as emerging markets. For the typical investor with limited means, this investment mix—domestic bonds and real estate and a stock portfolio incorporating both foreign market and domestic equities—may be the perfect combination. But for those with substantial assets of perhaps $1 million or more, we believe an all-inclusive portfolio, including emerging-market debt, real estate, and natural resources deserves attention as well.

The affluent global bargain hunter carries something that every emerging market craves: money, or, as economists prefer to call it, capital. Capital is in great demand in emerging markets, given the tremendous need to fund the development of infrastructure. Taiwan, with its desperate need for improved roads and new housing, is a case in point. The Taipei-to-Kaohsiong highway is called the "largest parking lot in the world" because the bumper-to-bumper traffic barely moves during rush hour. (A former student of ours who is currently a Taiwan University professor usually spends four hours every day on his twenty-mile commute to work.) Cities in emerging-market countries are so crowded with people that it is sometimes impossible to walk at your own pace—you are constantly pushed forward or restrained by the crowd behind or in front. There are so many people living in the cities of China that, according to a study by Prudential Real Estate Investors, 27 billion square feet of housing needs to be constructed in the next ten years to shelter the growing population. To be sure, supply can sometimes get ahead of effective demand, as appeared to be the case in 1997 in Beijing and Shanghai. But in the long run, we are convinced that a large growth in supply will be absorbed.

Rising population and robust economic growth have also created a huge demand for natural resources. Bombay, Shanghai, Taipei, and other industrial cities are today burning so much oil and coal that the smog has made it hard for people to see the sun even on a cloudless day. The implications are clear: the demand for debt to finance infrastructure projects will continue to grow; rising population will make land even more scarce in the cities; and the markets for natural resources, such as oil, water, cotton, and industrial materials, will become tighter as rising demands compete for limited supplies. These important trends in emerging markets are likely to provide some unprecedented investment opportunities for the most affluent global bargain hunters.

Emerging-Market Debt

The Case for Investing in Emerging-Market Debt

The rationale for investing in bonds or IOUs issued by emerging-market companies or governments is similar to that for investing in emerging-market equities: higher potential returns and greater risk reduction benefits resulting from diversification. According to a study conducted by Brinson Partners, the J. P. Morgan Emerging Market Bond Index (EMBI) generated an 11 percent return over and above that on U.S. Treasury bills from 1991 through 1995. Even larger returns were earned in 1996, as is shown in Figure 10-1. The EMBI's performance is comparable to that of the S&P 500 Index during the same period. Since the EMBI has almost no correlation with the world government bond index (which is made up mostly of U.S. and Japanese bonds), emerging-market bonds are an excellent addition to a diversified portfolio. While the defaulted Russian railroad bonds described in Chapter Three clearly show that holding *only* emerging-market bonds is too risky, the Brinson Partners study shows that for investors with enough resources to diversify very broadly, a careful mixture of emerging-market debt in a global securities portfolio can significantly improve the risk/return trade-off.

FIGURE 10-1

JP Morgan Emerging Market Bond Index

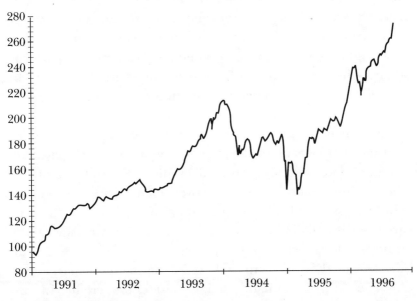

SOURCE: DATASTREAM

How to Evaluate Emerging-Market Debt

There are three factors to take into account when buying bonds: credit risk, general interest rate levels, and bond traders' psychology. Credit risk is the most important. In financial circles, credit risk means the likelihood of default; this, in turn, is determined by the issuer's capacity and willingness to service its debt. Capability and willingness tend to change over time according to each country's political and economic conditions. The Mexican debt crisis, for example, was triggered by internal political turmoil and the subsequent unwillingness of world investors to continue to refinance the government's short-term debt. What was disastrous for Mexican bonds, however, created only a short-term blip in bonds of other countries. It is precisely because emerging-market countries have yet to mesh into a seamless world economy that the long-term correlation of credit risks remains quite small across political entities. Thus, while the Mexican crisis certainly had an immediate effect on the bond markets of other emerging-market countries, most of them recovered quickly while Mexico struggled to attract international investors once more. Again, diversification is the magic word; with it, much default risk can be eliminated.

Paraphrasing George Orwell, some bonds are more equal than others. The most liquid of all emerging-market debt is the multibillion-dollar Brady bond market. Named after former U.S. Treasury Secretary Nicholas Brady, Brady bonds are unique emerging-market debt instruments issued to replace defaulted sovereign bank loans of developing countries. Their payments consist of two parts: one secured by the U.S. government, the other by the emerging-market government. The secured part (which often includes initial interest payments as well as the principal) has essentially zero credit risk because it is typically backed by short- or long-term U.S. government bonds. The sovereign part is backed by the "full faith and credit" of emerging-market governments, and this usually carries considerable credit risk. Because at least some of the payment is secured by U.S. bonds, however, Brady bonds are generally less risky than pure sovereign debt. Moreover, since most Brady bonds are dollar-denominated with all payments made in U.S. dollars, they have no direct exposure to currency risk. As a result, they have become a very popular debt instrument among world investors, accounting for 61 percent of emerging-market debt trading.

What of the remaining 39 percent? The good news is that even these riskier debt instruments, when broadly diversified through their purchase via a bond mutual fund, can play a role for those seeking portfolios of diversified assets. Four factors contribute to our optimistic prognosis. First, with the fall of communism, governments all over the world must now rely on markets to raise development capital and can no longer afford to pursue a costly policy of economic isolation. This tends to give governments a powerful incentive to honor financial obligations so that they may have continued access to world capital and technology. Second, the movement toward democracy in many emerging markets increased the hope for greater long-term political stability. We believe it is possible that revolution-caused defaults, such as Russia's in 1917, are now less likely. Third, the presence of the World Bank and the International Monetary Fund (IMF) as "lenders of last resort" may also help alleviate short-term liquidity crises that could lead to default. Fourth, the monitoring activities of these international organizations tend to increase the confidence of investors that the monetary and fiscal policies undertaken by individual countries will be appropriate.

The second factor in evaluating the attractiveness of bonds is the general interest rate level in the world market. Given the fact that emerging-market debt competes with other debt instruments for investors' capital, a rise in the general world interest rate level tends to raise the required rate of return on emerging-market debt. Already-issued IOUs, which have fixed long-term interest rate promises, must then fall in price to make them as attractive as newly issued IOUs at higher interest rates. Therefore, if U.S. interest rates rise, there will be a tendency for rates to increase all over the world.

The last factor is the human one: bond traders' psychology.

Bond traders are not computers that simply calculate the yields offered by different debt instruments and print out buy and sell orders. They are emotional human beings driven by greed, gambling instinct, hope, and fear in their bond investment decisions. Hope of very high returns can send bond prices soaring, leaving little protection for the default risk. Equally, fear of being left holding worthless wallpaper can lead to panic selling, producing very attractive returns for the patient and the brave. As shown in Figure 10-2, euphoria in emerging markets drove the yield spread on Brady bonds (the yield offered over and above the yield on perfectly safe U.S. Treasury bonds) to as little as 2.5 percentage points (250 basis points) in December 1993. The pessimism that pervaded emerging bond markets after the Mexican crisis sent the yield spread to as high as 10 percentage points in the first quarter of 1995. Thus, when U.S. Treasury yields were about 7 percent, emerging-market Brady bonds yielded about 17 percent. Even if the annual default turned out to be 10 percent, a well-diversified portfolio of Brady bonds would still have produced a decent yield of 10.3 percent.[1] Thus, global bargain hunters should not restrict their investments to equities. Bond investments can be extremely rewarding as well. While spreads were again relatively narrow in early 1997, it is clear that very attractive opportunities often exist in the emerging bond markets.

How to Invest in Emerging-Market Bonds

While it is possible for individuals to buy Brady bonds directly, the typical minimum purchase price of $10,000 means that obtaining a diversified portfolio of such bonds can be costly. By far the best and most practical route is to buy an emerging-market bond fund diversified throughout a region or, better still, around the world. The T. Rowe Price Emerging Markets Bonds fund listed in the first

---

1. Ninety percent of the portfolio would return 17 percent, while the 10 percent of the portfolio that defaulted would yield –50 percent, assuming that the defaulted bonds fall to half their former value.

FIGURE 10-2

Yeild Spreads: Brady Bonds vs. Comparable Treasuries
End of Month Yields, January 31, 1991 – January 31, 1997

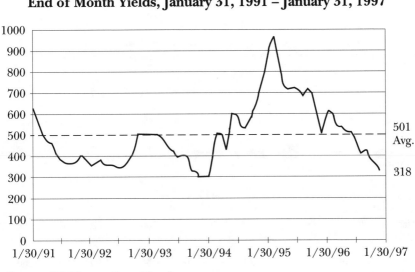

SOURCE: J.P. Morgan Securities, Inc.

section of Table 10-1, for example, is a well-diversified (open-end) mutual fund that can be purchased directly from the issuer without a sales charge (it is a no-load fund). The minimum initial purchases for regular accounts and IRAs are $2,500 and $1,000 respectively. Two other open-end bond funds are also listed in the table.

In addition, the table presents four closed-end funds that were available in early 1997 at a discount from the value of the bonds carried in their portfolios. These funds are similar to the closed-end funds described in Chapter Seven except that they hold bonds rather than stocks. The closed-end funds listed here are all traded on the New York Stock Exchange and can be purchased through any broker. Their advantage is that they can often be bought at a discount from their NAV (the market value of the bonds in their portfolio), as is the case for three of the funds in the table. Investors need to keep an eye on the discounts for emerging-market bond funds; these can be found each Monday in *The Wall Street Journal* (see Table 7-2). In general, funds with modest expense ratios and substantial discounts are more attractive.

TABLE 10-1

Open-End and Closed-End Emerging-Market Bond Funds, Early 1997*

Fund Name	Total Return, Previous 12 Months (%)	Market Price	Discount	Yield (%)	Average Maturity (Years)	Percentage of Fund in Brady Bonds	Expense Ratio	Leverage	Telephone Number
Open-end funds:									
Fidelity New Markets Income	32.11	$10.68	NA	8.9	15.9	94	1.17	No	(800) 544-888
Scudder Emerging Markets Inc.	31.43	12.09	NA	9.8	NA	93	1.50	No	(800) 225-247
T. Rowe Price Emerging Markets Bonds	25.81	11.04	NA	9.0	14.5	65	1.25	No	(800) 225-513
Closed-end funds:									
Emerging Markets Floating Rate	40.88	16⅜	(0.8)†	11.0	10.0	100	1.65	Yes	(800) 725-666
Latin America Dollar Income	28.05	14⅜	10.3	11.2	14.4	56	1.96	Yes	(800) 349-428
Morgan Stanley Emerging Markets Debt	35.60	13½	6.1	12.3	18.3	42	1.89	Yes	(800) 221-672
Templeton Emerging Markets Income	18.69	12½	9.2	10.6	9.8	41	0.81	No	(800) 292-929

*The numbers reported here are for reference only. They are subject to change as fund manage rebalance their portfolios.

†Parentheses indicate a premium.

SOURCE: *Morningstar Closed-End Fund 250,* 1996–1997 edition, and authors' telephone survey. Th expense ratios are the latest reported ratios.

Factors to consider in choosing an emerging-market bond fund are expense ratio, interest rate sensitivity, leverage, yield, and the credit quality of the bonds held in the portfolio. The expense ratio is one of the most important factors. Long-term studies of fund returns consistently confirm that funds with higher expenses tend to earn lower net returns. When you begin serious exploration of emerging-market bond funds, use this ratio to eliminate candidates. If a fund's expense ratio is above 2 percent, do not buy it.

Another factor to consider is interest rate sensitivity. All bonds are sensitive to interest rate changes. Emerging-market bonds have to compete with bonds from developed countries for investors' money. If world interest rates rise, emerging-market bonds need to offer higher yields to attract investment dollars. Therefore, the price of already-outstanding bonds with fixed interest payments must fall to provide larger returns in the future. In general, the longer the maturity of the bond fund, the more sensitive it is to interest rate changes. The average effective maturity of the funds in Table 10-1, for example, varies from 9.8 years to 18.3 years. Bond funds with longer maturities tend to be riskier.

Some funds may also use leverage to enhance their performance. What this means is that the funds may borrow from banks to increase their bets in the market. The operation is akin to buying stocks on margin. While the strategy may pay off handsomely if it works, it could also lead to significant losses if the manager makes a wrong bet. Generally, the higher the leverage ratio (money borrowed against NAV), the riskier the fund. Of the closed-end funds listed, the Templeton fund is the only one that does not use borrowing to enhance its performance.

All the funds listed in Table 10-1 offer fairly high yields. It is worth noting, however, that one should not always choose the funds with the highest yields. These tempting figures could reflect the fact that the fund has a longer maturity (greater interest rate risk). A high yield may also reflect poor credit quality. Generally, the lower the credit quality of the bond, the higher the yield. You may be taking more interest rate and/or credit risk by choosing a higher-yield fund. Funds that have a larger proportion of Brady bonds tend to be safer because the principal payments of the bonds are guaranteed by the U.S. government.

During the history of the closed-end funds listed in the table, the discounts on the funds have ranged from 13 percent to a premium of 22 percent. Recent financial studies have confirmed that funds with deep discounts have higher expected future returns than funds without discounts and funds selling at a premium. While the variation of discounts could to some extent be attributed to changing risk, our view is that occasional deep discounts may also reveal an unexploited market opportunity. Our advice is to buy closed-end funds only when they are selling at an unusually deep discount. At such times, you may not only get a higher current yield but also reap substantial capital gains if the discount narrows. This strategy is certainly not foolproof, since discounts can get deeper and NAV can also drop as a result of rising interest rates and increasing default risk. Our strategy, however, does put the odds in your favor.

Emerging-Market Real Estate

The Case for Investing in Emerging-Market Real Estate

If you have a substantial portfolio, we suggest that you also consider putting some funds into emerging-market properties, which is made possible through the purchase of property company ADRs. We do so for several reasons. First, over the long run, ownership of emerging-market real estate has produced generous rates of return that are comparable to those from common stocks and well above real estate returns in most developed countries. Figure 10-3 illustrates this point.

Equally important, real estate is an excellent vehicle to provide the benefits of diversification described in Chapter Six. It does this in two ways. First, real estate returns have a relatively low correlation with other assets, such as stocks. Second, real estate returns in one part of the world are generally not correlated with those in others. As Figure 10-3 suggests, during the 1988–1994 period, when the West and Japan were suffering through one of the worst real estate slumps in history, emerging markets were enjoying a boom. The average correlations between the United States

FIGURE 10-3

Average Annual Rates of Capital Appreciation on Real Estate (in US Dollars) 1988–1994

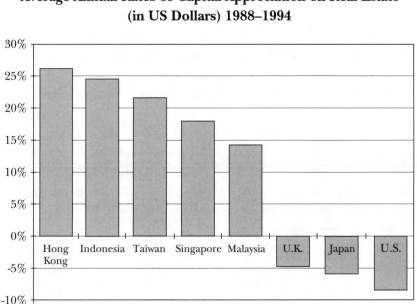

SOURCE: Daniel Quan and Sheridan Titman, "Commercial Real Estate Prices and Stock Market Returns: An International Analysis."

and five Asian real estate markets in a study by Daniel Quan and Sheridan Titman were actually negative during the time period covered. Thus, putting some share of your portfolio into emerging-market properties can reduce the overall risk of your investment program.

There is an additional advantage: real estate has often been a fairly reasonable hedge against inflation in emerging markets. During periods of double-digit inflation in Hong Kong and other parts of Asia, real estate returns were considerably higher than the rate of inflation and even higher than the returns from the broad stock market indices in several countries.

All of these real estate investment factors—generous rates of return, risk reduction through diversification, and a hedge against inflation—make emerging-market real estate attractive. Moreover, in early 1997, many real estate companies appeared to be priced more moderately than other blue-chip common stocks in emerging markets. The P/E ratio for many Hong Kong property companies was around 14, somewhat below that of the Hong Kong stock market index (the Hang Seng index). In the past, any moderation of the P/E ratios of property companies has provided an excellent opportunity for investors to build up their position in real estate assets.

Long-term fundamentals are particularly bright as far as real estate investment is concerned. First, there is a housing crisis in almost all of the major cities in developing nations. For example, according to official Chinese statistics, in 1995 the average living space for a family of four in Shanghai was about 400 square feet. Many families have only one bedroom, so that parents have to sleep in the same room with their grown children. With the exception of some new high-rise apartment buildings in major cities, many apartments do not have private amenities, such as toilets, running water, and stoves. The situation is even worse in Bombay. More than half of its 14 million residents live on the street or in slums with no access to running water or electricity. A family of six would be considered very lucky if it could live in a 280-square-foot public housing unit. There is no doubt that, with increased income and a free housing market, residents in emerging markets will spend a significant amount of money to improve their dreadful housing conditions.

Second, demographic factors in emerging markets are likely to create a strong demand for housing. According to Jim Rohwer, a CS First Boston Chief Economist, in his book *Asia Rising*, "Of the 3.3 billion Asians alive in 1995, some 1.7 billion, or around 52 percent, are under the age of 25. Only 35 percent of Americans and 28 percent of Germans are that young." Over the next twenty years, most of these 1.7 billion people will find jobs, get married, and start families. Twenty-five years ago, the young families might have chosen to squeeze into an apartment with their parents. With increasing income, however, they will probably prefer to live on their own. This suggests a substantial increase in demand for affordable housing by these young families.

Third, rapid industrialization and poor infrastructure (roads, electric and telephone service, etc.) in rural areas have led to massive urbanization in developing countries. According to a U.N. study, by the end of 2015, nine out of the ten largest cities in the world will be in emerging markets and none will be in the United States (see Table 10-2). Massive migration from rural areas to urban centers will exacerbate housing problems in these cities. For example, it is estimated that about 100 million Chinese migrant workers will be working in cities in 1998. Many emerging markets are already densely populated, as shown in Table 10-3. India, for example, has almost *ten times* the population density of the United States. South Korea is even more densely populated. Any further migration to cities would make urban land an increasingly scarce resource.

TABLE 10-2

U.N. Estimates of the World's Largest Cities in 2015

Rank	City	Country	Population, 1994 (in millions)	Population, 2015 (in millions)	Growth, 1994–2015 (%)
1	Tokyo	Japan	26.5	28.7	8
2	Bombay	India	14.5	27.4	89
3	Lagos	Nigeria	9.7	24.4	152
4	Shanghai	China	14.7	23.4	59
5	Jakarta	Indonesia	11.0	21.2	93
6	São Paulo	Brazil	16.1	20.8	29
7	Karachi	Pakistan	9.5	20.6	117
8	Beijing	China	12.0	19.4	62
9	Dacca	Bangladesh	7.4	19.0	157
10	Mexico City	Mexico	15.5	18.8	21

SOURCE: United Nations, *Urban Agglomerations 1994.*

TABLE 10-3

**U.N. Estimates of the Growing Urbanization
of Various Countries**

Country	Population (in millions)	Density (people per sq. km.)	Urban Population as a Percentage of Total Population 1992	2000
Argentina	34	12	87	89
Brazil	164	18	76	81
Chile	14	18	84	85
China	1,215	120	28	35
India	928	264	26	29
Malaysia	20	55	51	57
Mexico	89	43	74	78
Philippines	68	210	51	59
South Korea	45	437	77	86
Thailand	61	111	19	22
United States	265	27	76	78

SOURCE: United Nations, *Urban Agglomerations 1994.*

There is ample evidence that a scarcity of urban land has already made emerging-market cities some of the most expensive places in the world to live and do business in. According to a *New York Times* study in July 1995, the average rent of a decent two-bedroom apartment was $1,500 per month in Buenos Aires, $5,000 in Moscow, $6,300 in Shanghai, $7,100 in Hong Kong, and $7,800 in Bombay. The notoriously high rent in New York ($2,300) was actually a bargain by emerging-market standards.

Trying to make the maximum use of existing land, more and more developers are reaching to the sky. The tallest buildings in the world are now in Asia rather than in the United States. Thanks to a decorative spire, the Petronas Towers in Kuala Lumpur (pictured in Chapter Two) are 9 meters (29 feet) taller than the Sears Tower in Chicago, previously the world's tallest building. When completed, the World Financial Center in Shanghai (see drawing) will be even taller, as shown in Table 10-4.

TABLE 10-4

Building Castles in the Air: The World's Tallest Buildings

Building	Location	Height (meters)	Number of Stories	Year of Completion
World Financial Center	Shanghai	460	95	—
Petronas Towers	Kuala Lumpur	450	85	1996
Sears Tower	Chicago	443	110	1974
Jinmao Tower	Shanghai	420	88	1996
World Trade Center	New York City	417	110	1970
Commercial Center	Shenzhen	383	81	—
Empire State Building	New York City	381	102	1931
Central Plaza	Hong Kong	374	78	1992
Bank of China Tower	Hong Kong	368	77	1989

SOURCE: *Asiaweek; Overseas Chinese Daily.*

Finally, real estate should profit handsomely from rapidly rising real wages. Property construction is very labor intensive, and the cost of construction labor in many countries is rising rapidly. Between 1991 and 1993, the cost of labor rose by more than 57 percent in China, 22 percent in Mexico, and 20 percent in Korea in dollar terms. Given this rapid rise in real wages, an office building that costs $200 million to construct today might cost twice as much in less than five years. If the market value of the building reflects its replacement cost, an investor today could reap a capital gain of 100 percent in five years simply by taking advantage of rising labor costs.

In summary, with continued economic growth and favorable demographic trends for the next twenty years, property companies with a large land reserve and adequate capital should be very well positioned to take advantage of the surging demand we anticipate. As a result, many of these companies may be able to generate above-average rates of return for their shareholders.

**Artist's Rendering of the Planned
World Financial Center in Shanghai**

The Case Against Emerging-Market Real Estate

It is important to recognize that emerging-market real estate is highly speculative. Most real estate developers are prone to excess. During the 1980s, there was excessive development all over the world—in Tokyo, London, California, Hawaii, and Texas. The favorite game was always to see who could build the tallest office tower in town or the most luxurious apartments or hotels in the area. While the party lasted, it was fun for everyone; when it ended, bankers and investors were stuck with huge bills. Overbuilding in Japan, for instance, caused Tokyo real estate prices to plummet by two-thirds to three-fourths from their peak in the late 1980s, while wild speculation and excess building in Texas led to the failure of hundreds of savings and loans.

Indeed, it is the wildness of real estate markets that restrains our enthusiasm somewhat. While the long-term picture may be bright, this is an area where inappropriate timing can lead to quite unsatisfactory investment results. In Japan's bubble economy of the late 1980s, financial gurus used to walk through Tokyo and count the number of construction cranes that filled the city streets. At the time, this "crane index," along with its more disreputable cousin, the "erection index" (the height of the tallest building under construction), was optimistically viewed as an augury of the virility of the bull market in real estate. Unfortunately, this augury signaled an impending collapse of the market. Very often, the completion of the world's tallest skyscraper has coincided with a market peak.

Today, the real estate party has moved to the world of emerging markets. From Bangkok to East Berlin and from Shenzhen to Seoul, armies of construction workers are working on roads, apartment blocks, office buildings, shopping malls, and golf courses. While many of these developments have undoubtedly filled large demand gaps, excessive development has also produced a glut of vacant space and see-through (unleased) buildings in many "hot" places. According to Shanghai government estimates, in 1994 the total stock of central business district office space was only 2.3 million square feet. It jumped by 9 million square feet in 1995 and further increased by another staggering 32 million square feet in 1996. That is equivalent to ten Empire State Buildings of new office space in just two years! As a result, the office vacancy rate skyrocketed from 1 percent in 1994, to more than 50 percent in 1996, and rents in Shanghai have fallen by more than 40 percent.

To reduce such speculative risk, we suggest that investors avoid the most lavish development projects. You may miss a lot of fun, but you could also avoid paying huge bills. What matters in the end is the size of your returns, not the height of your trophy buildings. One useful measure for identifying speculative crazes in real estate is the ratio of the market value of a property to what it would cost to replace the building. A high market-to-replacement ratio (much greater than 1) means that it will pay a developer to acquire land in the neighborhood and build a similar building and implies an increasing supply of space and more competition. Investors in buildings selling above replacement cost can get stuck with a double loss: falling rents and falling property market value. On the other hand, investors buying during a real estate recession, when the market-to-replacement ratio is much smaller than 1, can get a double benefit. If demand for space picks up, it means rising rents and increasing property values.

One positive feature that somewhat mitigates the risks is that the property cycles of emerging markets are likely to be shorter than those in developed markets if these markets continue their high economic growth. For example, if Shanghai maintains its 15 percent growth rate in the absorption of space, then even with a 50 percent vacancy rate, it would still achieve full occupancy in about four years. On the other hand, it may take a typical American city seven to ten years to fill a 20 percent vacancy if the local economy is growing at only 2 to 3 percent a year. Given the difficulty in supplying new space on short notice, it may even be rational, in some emerging markets, to build in anticipation of future demand.

Another source of risk often cited is the changing business environment. Many observers have suggested that emerging-market economies may get more suburban, as happened in the United States, leaving many downtown buildings with large amounts of vacant space. While this may become true in the future, we expect that it will take quite a long time because of the personal nature of business transactions in many emerging markets. Given the poor transportation infrastructure in most emerging economies, downtown is still the most efficient place for doing business, and we do not expect that to change soon.

In addition to speculative and business risks, political risk is also a major source of concern for investors. Given its immobility, real estate is very vulnerable to government expropriation and excessive taxes. An obvious case is Hong Kong. With a 15 percent flat tax rate, a highly reliable legal system, and a relatively unintrusive government, Hong Kong has flourished as the region's financial center, and its real estate commands the highest rents and prices in the world. Will China continue to keep the world's most successful capitalist system intact now that it has taken over Hong Kong? Will the development of Chinese cities such as Shanghai and Shenzhen steal the thunder away from Hong Kong? These are major uncertainties facing today's investors.

While real estate bulls correctly argue that valuation levels in terms of price-to-cash-flow or P/E ratios were still quite reasonable in Hong Kong in early 1997, whether these cash flow levels can be safely projected into the future is far more doubtful. As a popular saying in Hong Kong goes, "You cannot predict a Chinese future based on a British past." However, history is on the side of Hong Kong. China desperately needs Hong Kong's financial support and access to the world market. It is in China's self-interest to keep Hong Kong a "princess of capitalism" rather than turning her back into Cinderella. As a result, we can accept the cautiously optimistic case about the future of Hong Kong. Our view is that a *small* Hong Kong real estate position could help investors diversify portfolio risk and improve expected returns. But we would certainly caution against overexposure.

How to Invest in Emerging-Market Real Estate

Most individuals lack both the expertise to evaluate emerging-market property investments and the large sums required to purchase them. Moreover, poor liquidity and high transactions costs make it very difficult to turn a property investment into cash if an emergency funding requirement arises or the investment prospects change. Thus, given the absence of real estate investment trusts (REITs) in emerging markets, property company stocks listed as ADRs offer the only practical vehicle for individual investors in the United States to add emerging-market real estate to their portfolios.

There are a few dozen property and hotel company ADRs with relatively good trading markets. During the mid-1990s, many Hong Kong developers, such as Hopewell Holdings and New World, have poured capital into China, India, Indonesia, Malaysia, and Thailand. Thus, investors can obtain property interests in South Asia just by purchasing Hong Kong property company shares. These shares are traded like regular stocks, and they are covered by many international accounting firms, so that company financial information is easily available (see Table 10-5). However, some of these companies are not traded on major stock exchanges, and their accounting information may not always conform exactly to U.S. standards.

It is worth noting that if you have invested in one of the emerging-market equity funds described in previous chapters, you will already have some exposure to emerging-market real estate, as the portfolios of these funds usually include some real estate securities. Thus, many investors will not need to purchase property company shares directly. But since this exposure tends to be small—usually no more than 10 percent of the fund's assets—you may wish to increase your real estate holdings if you are very optimistic about the long-term effects of economic and population growth. Moreover, real estate in such countries as Argentina, Brazil, India, Indonesia, Malaysia, and Thailand is underrepresented in many funds.

TABLE 10-5

Property ADRs Traded in the United States

Company	Country	Price	P/E Ratio	P/BV Ratio	Yield (%)	Earnings Growth Rate, 1991– 1995
Amoy Properties	Hong Kong	$5.80	13.5	0.81	4.74	13.7%
Bandar Raya Development	Malaysia	1.55	15.5	2.42	1.59	50.9
Cheung Kong	Hong Kong	7.36	11.3	2.89	2.11	29.6
Hang Lung	Hong Kong	9.55	9.0	0.94	4.64	13.9
Henderson Land	Hong Kong	7.14	12.2	2.46	3.44	32.2
Hopewell Holdings	Hong Kong	2.91	15.0	0.73	2.89	—
IRSA	Argentina	26.80	12.1	1.18	3.35	—
Israel Land	Israel	8.25	18.3	—	0.00	20.1
Malayan Credit	Singapore	2.11	29.9	1.05	1.16	27.0
New World	Hong Kong	9.03	16.4	1.23	3.09	18.6
Singapore Land	Singapore	7.02	40.0	1.08	0.70	28.1
Sun Hung Kai	Hong Kong	9.50	16.1	1.78	2.41	26.1

SOURCE: Morningstar, *International Stocks, 1996.*

We also believe that large institutional investors will be well served by adding some emerging-market properties to their real estate portfolios. If these admittedly risky properties are combined with real estate in developed countries, the low correlation of their returns can actually *reduce* the overall risk of the portfolio. Institutions should diversify not only across different countries but also across different property types. Portfolio managers may do so by investing in shares of local companies or by taking an equity position in some development projects.

Other Investment Opportunities

The substantial economic growth we anticipate for emerging markets and the increased incomes we project for their huge populations imply that the real (adjusted for general inflation) prices of commodities, such as oil, grain, rubber, and metals, will rise in the future. This projection is further supported by the fact that the real prices of many commodities, such as oil, are below their historical levels for the last twenty-five years. Commodities are also found to have low correlations with equities and bonds, making them good additions to a diversified portfolio. Our preference is to invest in a natural resource equity fund rather than in a fund investing in commodity futures. The reason for this choice is that equity funds generally enjoy the same benefits as commodity funds but tend to have lower expense ratios. (We always prefer putting money to work for ourselves to paying for fund managers' yachts.) Table 10-6 presents a sample of natural resource equity funds that meet our general criteria for investment.

Given the rapid increase in the number of millionaires and billionaires expected in emerging markets, some advisers argue that it makes sense to invest in local art, antiques, rare coins, stamps, and other collectibles. After all, many collectibles are in limited supply while the number of rich people is growing exponentially. Enthusiasts like to point out, for example, that the returns from investing in Chinese ceramics have exceeded those from the S&P 500 during the past twenty-five years, and they have also had a low correlation with other asset classes. Our view, however, is that unless you really love them for their own sake, collectibles are not an effective investment medium. Fakes and forgeries are common, commissions are enormous, and collectibles tend to be terribly illiquid. Moreover, over time they collect dust instead of dividends.

In conclusion, the presence of emerging-market debt, real estate, and natural resources has provided global bargain hunters with adventursome new opportunities. For those with substantial assets, a diversified portfolio that includes these investments could make the adventure more rewarding and less risky.

TABLE 10-6

Selected Natural Resource Mutual Funds

Fund Name	Total Return Annualized, Five Years to 1997	Morningstar Rating	Foreign Stocks (%)	Net Assets (in millions)	Load Fee (%)	Expense Ratio (%)	Minimum Initial Purchase	Minimum Initial IRA Purchase	Telephone Number
Fidelity Advisor Global Resources A	17.89	***	21.4	$484.5	3.50	1.84	$2,500	$500	(800) 522-7297
Fidelity Select Industrial Materials	15.95	***	34.8	130.9	3.00	1.53	2,500	500	(800) 544-8888
T. Rowe Price New Era	14.81	***	21.3	1,306.8	0.00	0.79	2,500	1,000	(800) 638-5660
Vanguard Specialized Energy	10.59	***	27.1	612.1	0.00	0.48	3,000	1,000	(800) 662-7447

SOURCE: Morningstar.

CHAPTER ELEVEN

Investment Strategies and Specific Recommendations

"LIFE IS LIKE a box of chocolates—you never know what you're gonna get." Although these words of wisdom are from the fictional Forrest Gump's mother, they could well be the motto for those investing in individual emerging markets. Despite the overall appeal of extraordinary growth and attractive selling prices, there's no way of knowing what return you will get from any single market or region. The risks of concentrating in just one of these areas are enormous.

And yet, despite the acknowledged financial danger, a diversified holding of emerging-market securities both lowers risk and increases expected returns. Emerging-market investments are not only for the daring and the brave—they should be basic portfolio components for the proverbial "widows and orphans" as well. In fact, we believe that U.S. investors should put as much as 40 percent of their common stock holdings into foreign markets and that approximately one-third of this exposure (up to 13 percent of total investments) should be in emerging markets.

But before you start your global bargain hunt, we offer some final broad investment advice. First, we sum up many of the themes of this book with one contrarian and three cardinal investing rules—all tailored to an emerging-market strategy. Finally, we "name names" and give you specific recommendations for asset allocation by general life cycle, and under each we recommend specific funds to purchase.

General Investment Rules

Rule 1: Stay Cool

The press is forever writing about "the investment manager with the hot hand," "the most attractive emerging markets for your investment dollars today," or "the most spectacular emerging-market fund" for the current year. Skip over these headlines. Diversification eschews chasing after the "hottest" country funds reported in magazines and newspapers. The best performing funds tend to concentrate in similar geographic regions or industries. By purchasing last year's top-performing funds, you are likely to end up with a poorly diversified portfolio. Moreover, last year's "hottest" funds may include stocks with high valuation levels that may not be sustainable. Finally, there is no evidence that past winners will be future winners. Indeed, there is a strong tendency in mutual fund returns for regression to the mean. You are not likely to improve your results by purchasing last period's best performers.

Rule 2: Diversify Broadly

Life on the emerging-market investment frontier is truly wild—it is a jungle with few rules of fair play. Risk is not easy to measure or project, and real risk must often be experienced the hard way. Robert Kirby, another legendary professional investor, recounts the story of a young Chinese boy who learned that lesson all too well:

> The boy lived on a farm in a rural area of China. One day, being bored and having nothing much to do, he yielded to an urge to push the family outhouse off the edge of the ravine on which it stood. A while later his father came up and asked, "Chang, did you push the outhouse into the ravine?"
>
> Chang answered, "No, Father, I did not."
>
> The father said, "Chang, I would like to tell you the story of George Washington, who was the first and one of the most revered leaders of our new friends, the Americans."

He told Chang the story of the cherry tree and how George Washington was rewarded for telling the truth. Upon finishing, he once again asked Chang, "Did you push the privy into the ravine?"

This time, Chang answered, "Yes, Father, I cannot tell a lie. I did."

The father thereupon thrashed Chang to within an inch of his life. After Chang finally gathered himself together, he asked, "But, Father, what about George Washington and the cherry tree?"

Chang's father replied, "My son, there was one big difference. George Washington's father was not in the cherry tree when he cut it down."

As we have repeatedly warned, the investor who purchases securities in emerging markets accepts many special risks. These markets are extraordinarily volatile, and, particularly when certain countries or regions become extremely popular, investors can easily overpay for their stocks. Moreover, the quality of accounting information and the ethical standards of business behavior sometimes leave much to be desired. History is full of examples of sovereign governments breaking their promises to investors and expropriating private property. Political and currency risks are substantial, and it is costly and difficult to sell one's holdings in illiquid emerging markets.

There is no way that investment risks can be eliminated, but we have stressed that the one sure way of mitigating these risks is to diversify broadly across countries. It is extremely difficult to predict the returns from different emerging markets. Thus we suggest that you diversify broadly by purchasing an emerging-markets index fund or a broad group of individual funds, ensuring that your portfolio is roughly diversified according to the relative size of the economies in different regions.

Rule 3: Check Out Investment Bargains

There are two crucial value factors that global bargain hunters must consider when they purchase emerging-market security funds: expense ratios and discounts.

As discussed in Chapter Seven, mutual fund annual expense charges vary from less than 0.5 percent to more than 3 percent per year. These charges come out of any return you might earn (and, in some cases, compound your losses). You may also pay an up-front sales charge (or load fee) as well. At first glance, you might think you get what you pay for. You might believe that the fund charging 3 percent must give better service or, more important, better performance over time. Unfortunately, those beliefs are wrong. Overall, there is no relationship between a fund's expense ratio and its success in picking investments. In fact, the passively managed emerging-markets index we recommended in Chapter Eight has outperformed almost all of the actively managed funds. And the Vanguard index fund charges the lowest annual expenses, approximately 0.6 percent per year. We strongly advise making low expenses a major criterion in your investment decision. Never buy a fund with an expense ratio of more than 2 percent per year or with a high load or sales charge.

We also suggested that you can cash in on the equivalent of a major clearance sale when you buy closed-end funds selling at substantial discounts, as many did in early 1997. Investors should always check the weekly newspaper listings in papers such as *The Wall Street Journal,* where they appear each Monday. If you buy a closed-end fund at a 20 percent discount, you actually buy stocks on sale—$100 worth of stocks for $80. This is a bargain hunter's dream, especially when the funds have moderate expense ratios. When closed-end funds are available at substantial discounts, we prefer them to low-cost index funds.

Rule 4: Buy and Hold

Given the difficulty in forecasting returns from individual emerging markets, there is little reason to believe that a trading strategy involving high turnover will beat a simple strategy of buying and holding a diversified portfolio. On the other hand, the higher long-term growth that we project for emerging economies is likely to produce a long-term upswing in equity prices—although it could take time for these long-term gains to materialize. As a Hong Kong money manager pointed out, "China [or any other emerging market] may be the best opportunity of the decade, but only if you give it a decade."

We suggest two exceptions to our strictures against portfolio trading. If you have invested in a fund that has declined in price and selling it will allow you to take a tax deduction, selling and reinvesting the proceeds in an equivalent fund could make sense. The second exception involves selling to maintain diversification guidelines. Suppose your portfolio included a number of closed-end funds from different countries balanced to represent all emerging markets roughly in proportion to the size of their economies. Also suppose the appropriate weight for a particular country was 10 percent but speculative mania pushed the value of your holding in that country to 30 percent of your emerging-market portfolio. You could consider paring the holding down to perhaps 20 percent and keeping the overweighting within some guideline, such as no more than double the appropriate GDP weight. Such a strategy would have limited an investor's loss from the crash of the Taiwan market described in Part II.

Creating an Age-Appropriate Portfolio

American poet Margaret Fishback once called it "the same old charitable lie"—the phrase "You really haven't changed a bit." What with Rogaine, plastic surgery, contact lenses, and gleaming white tooth caps, perhaps you have not. As an investor, however, you cannot escape the steady onslaught of time. Younger investors (those in their twenties and thirties) can afford the extra risk inherent in securities because their incomes chiefly consist of wages. Older folks (and as baby boomers age, the definition of "older" tends to rise every year—gone forever is the slogan "Never trust anyone over thirty") pay an increasing proportion of their living expenses from investment income. By its very nature, loss of such income represents financial disaster. Thus, as investors enter their forties and fifties, portfolio composition begins to shift to more conservative financial instruments, with an emphasis on guaranteed income that will be needed in retirement.

Whether you are a younger or older investor, however, the chances are very high that your portfolio suffers from a "home-country bias"; that is, most of your money is concentrated in the United States. Even professional U.S. institutional investors held close to 95 percent of their equity funds in domestically domiciled stocks during the mid-1990s, with little investment in emerging markets. This implies that U.S. workers relying on their private employer or their state-sponsored pension plan for retirement savings are underexposed to emerging-market securities.

To help you determine what a reasonable allocation of your investments should be, Figure 11-1 provides recommendations on the general asset classes that are appropriate for investors in different age groups. Note that younger investors are advised to hold most of their assets in common stocks. Over long periods of time, stocks have provided far more generous rates of return than long-term bonds or cash investments (by which we mean bank savings accounts, certificates of deposit, and mutual fund money market accounts). While stocks tend to be far riskier than bank deposits or money market funds, young people will generally have a greater capacity to accept such risks. With the ability to earn wages from employment, people in their working years can maintain their standard of living in the face of stock market reverses. Moreover, younger investors saving for retirement will generally have long holding periods for their investments, and over long periods of time, such as twenty-five years, stocks have tended to provide generous rates of return.

Note that Figure 11-1 shows that as one ages, the recommended percentage of common stocks declines. A sixty-five-year-old widow in poor health does not have the capacity to earn income from employment. Hence, any reversal from her investments will immediately be reflected in her standard of living. This is why her recommended asset allocation concentrates on safer long-term bonds and short-term securities, which provides a dependable source of income, which can be obtained without incurring the transactions costs involved in selling securities. Table 11-1 outlines the specific percentages that are recommended for U.S. investors in each age group, along with suggestions on how investments in those asset classes might be allocated among specific instruments.

Figure 11-1

**Asset Allocation for Various Age Groups
Examples for U.S. Investors**

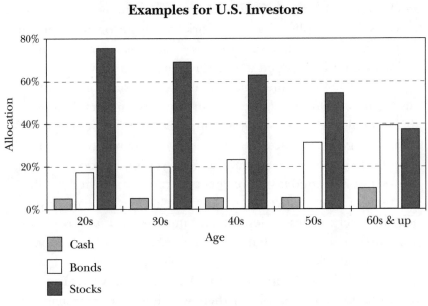

Table 11-1

Recommended Portfolio Compositions for Various Age Groups

All funds should be either no-load, low-expense mutual funds or closed-end funds available at discounts. Index funds are effective vehicles for both stock and bond investments.

Mid-twenties:

Cash (5%): Money market fund or short-term bond fund
Bonds (20%): 10% U.S. Treasury or high-grade corporate bond fund, 5% international bond fund, 5% emerging-market bond fund (e.g., Brady Bond Fund)

Stocks (75%):

    Domestic (45%): 20% diversified small-company fund, 25% diversified large-company fund*

    International (30%): 15% diversified international fund, 15% diversified emerging-market fund

Mid-thirties:

Cash (5%): Money market fund or short-term bond fund
Bonds (25%): 15% domestic bond funds, 10% foreign and emerging-market bond funds
Stocks (70%):

    Domestic (45%): 20% diversified small-company fund, 25% diversified large-company stock fund*

    International (25%): 12.5% diversified international fund, 12.5% diversified emerging-market fund

Mid-forties:

Cash (5%): Money market fund or short-term bond fund
Bonds (30%): 20% domestic bond funds, 10% foreign and emerging-market bond funds
Stocks (65%):

    Domestic (42.5%): 17.5% diversified small-company fund, 25% diversified large-company fund*

    International (22.5%): 12.5% diversified international fund, 10% diversified emerging-market fund

Mid-fifties:

Cash (5%): Money market fund or short-term bond fund
Bonds (40%): 30% domestic bond funds, 10% foreign and emerging-market bond funds
Stocks (55%):

    Domestic (35%): 12.5% diversified small-company fund, 22.5% diversified large-company fund*

    International (20%): 12.5% diversified international fund, 7.5% diversified emerging-market fund

Sixties and beyond:

Cash (10%): Money market fund or short-term bond fund

Bonds (50%): 40% domestic bond funds, 10% foreign and emerging-market bond funds
Stocks (40%):

     Domestic (30%): 10% diversified small-company fund, 20% diversified large-company fund*

     International (10%): 5% diversified international fund, 5% diversified emerging-market fund

---

*Some real estate exposure should be included within the equity portion of the portfolio. In the United States, this can be accomplished by purchasing a mutual fund holding a diversified portfolio of Real Estate Investment Trusts (REITs).

The general advice contained in Table 11-1 is that as one ages and the capacity for risk taking diminishes, the portfolio composition should become tilted toward safer and less volatile investments. Thus, the equity portion of the portfolio should shrink and more stable fixed-income investments should make up a larger share of the total. In all cases, however, we recommend that at least some part of the total be invested in emerging-market securities because of their diversification benefits. Of course, anyone may wish to make modest changes in the recommended percentages according to his or her individual risk tolerance and capacity for risk as determined by the dependability of other income, assets, or special circumstances. Ultimately, your program should allow you to feel secure and avoid bouts of anxiety and insomnia.[1]

To put more concreteness on these recommendations, we present in Table 11-2 a sample portfolio for Mr. and Mrs. Smith, a couple in their late forties. Mr. Smith is employed as a computer programmer, and Mrs. Smith is a high school teacher. Their combined income is $150,000 per year, their children have completed their schooling, and they hope to retire in fifteen to twenty years, when they are just past their sixty-fifth birthdays. Their assets total

---

1. Rebalancing one's portfolio with age might entail the payment of capital gains taxes, which could erode the value of one's assets. Investors should therefore be sure to hold any high-turnover investments in tax-deferred plans, such as 401(k)s.

$250,000. As this portfolio was drawn up in early 1997, some emerging-market closed-end investment funds were available at almost a 20 percent discount and are therefore suggested here as investments for the Smiths. Not since 1990 were such large discounts available to the investing public. Readers are cautioned, however, that discounts on these funds are very volatile. Closed-end funds are appropriate only if available at a substantial discount or if they are the only way of getting into a restricted market. Should the discount narrow or disappear, open-end (including open-end index) funds would be preferable.

TABLE 11-2

Portfolio for Mr. and Mrs. Smith
Ages: Late Forties
Assets: $250,000

Investments in Open-End Mutual Funds
and Closed-End Investment Companies

Type of Holding	*Amount*	*Fund*	*Comments*
Cash	$12,500	Fidelity Spartan Money Market Fund	A low-expense money market fund. If the Smith family is in a high tax bracket, a tax-exempt money market fund invested in securities of their home state should be used.
Bonds	$50,000	Vanguard Total Bond Market Index Fund*	An index fund diversified across the U.S. bond market.
	$12,500	T. Rowe Price International Bonds	A low-expense international fund diversified across non-U.S. bonds.
	$12,500	Templeton Emerging Markets Income Fund	A closed-end world income fund selling at a discount relative to its historical precedent.
Total bonds	$75,000		

Stocks (domestic)	$105,000	Vanguard Total Stock Market Index Fund*	An index fund designed to track the Wilshire 5000 total stock market index.
Stocks (international)	$32,500	T. Rowe Price International Stocks	A low-expense inter-national fund diversified across non-U.S. markets mostly European and Asia-Pacific stocks.
	$15,000	Vanguard Emerging Markets Index Fund*	An index fund designed to track the Morgan Stanley Capital Emerging Market Free Index.
	$5,000	Templeton Dragon Fund	A deep-discount closed-end fund designed to benefit mostly from the growth of Chinese companies in the Asia-Pacific region. The fund has some real estate stocks.
	$5,000	Czech Republic Fund	A closed-end fund invest-ing in a diversified port-folio of stocks in eastern Europe, including the Czech Republic, Hun-gary, and Poland.
Total (international)	$57,500		
Total Portfolio	$250,000		

*Note again that the first author of this book is a director of The Vanguard Group.

Here we have selected the Vanguard Emerging Markets Index Fund to form the core of our emerging-market holdings because it offers a low-expense way of building a widely diversified portfolio of emerging-market stocks. The fund does not have a sales fee, but it does impose a small transactions fee on the amount of new fund purchases and a 1 percent redemption fee for short-term holders to cover the high transactions costs. Note that we have supplemented the index fund with the Templeton Dragon Fund and the Czech Republic Fund. As discussed in Chapter Nine, China and eastern Europe are currently underrepresented in the Vanguard index fund. Adding the Dragon and Czech funds provides a more balanced portfolio. Overall, our portfolio appears to be slightly overweighted in the Asian markets because the market capitalization weights do not reflect the enormous size of the Asian economy. Moreover, there is some exposure to emerging-market real estate in these recommendations through funds which include real estate equities among their holdings.

A Final Word

Emerging-market investors should remember that just over a century ago the United States was still considered by rich Europeans to be a large emerging market. Investing in the United States was quite a risky venture. Financial fraud was rampant and default commonplace. Even the state of Mississippi defaulted on its bonds. After raising capital in Europe, many business promoters would return to the United States and never be heard from again. The country was vast, and transportation was poor. It would take several weeks of travel across the ocean for a European investor to come to the United States to check out his investments. The frontier was wild and lawless. A global bargain hunter in the United States sometimes literally needed to be a sharpshooter to get a return on his money. However, despite the huge risks, the United States emerged as the most powerful economy in the world, and investors earned generous real rates of return even after factoring out inflation.

By the same token, thirty years ago, Japan's economy was an emerging market (or reemerging market, to be more precise, since its development had been interrupted by World War II). After a devastating war, most of the country's physical capital was destroyed and the economy had to be built from ground zero. Short of oil and many other natural resources, Japan had to rely on foreign trade for its economic development. However, through its people's hard work and creativity, Japan produced an economic miracle that quickly put it into the league of developed nations. A $10,000 investment in a Japan fund in 1962 would have grown to approximately $1.5 million at the beginning of 1997, despite its lackluster performance in the early 1990s. This clearly demonstrates the point that while it is reckless to ignore the risks of emerging markets, it is equally irresponsible to ignore their growth opportunities.

Today, on the eve of the twenty-first century, as we survey the broad landscape of emerging markets, we find that the prospects for potential gains from the world's emerging economies are as good as at any other time in history. We are convinced that emerging markets will generate extremely generous returns for long-term investors. At the same time, investments in emerging markets may well yield tangible improvements in the everyday lives of billions of people around the world who must contend with difficult economic and social conditions. A narrowing of global economic disparities may, in turn, help to propel the world into a more peaceful and prosperous new millennium.

PART III HIGHLIGHTS:

1. Long-term investment is the key to financial success in emerging markets.

2. Adjust asset allocation and risk exposure according to your life-cycle investment objectives.

3. Use low-cost, low-turnover index funds as the "core" of a diversified international portfolio.

4. Closed-end funds are often available at substantial discounts from the value of the assets they hold. When you can buy assets at 80 to 85 cents on the dollar, it is time to open your wallet to closed-end funds.

5. Managed, open-end investment funds provide another investment alternative. Buy no-load, low-expense, low-turnover funds and avoid chasing "hot" funds with the best near-term records.

6. If you insist on actively managing your emerging-market investment portfolio, the rules in Chapter Nine should make the hunt for profits a bit less dangerous.

7. For those with substantial assets, emerging-market bonds, real estate, and natural resource securities can help round out your portfolio.

8. Emerging markets represent the most exciting investment opportunities for the twenty-first century, opportunities no investment portfolio should ignore.

References

We have resisted our academic proclivity to pepper the text with many footnotes and references. Our desire was to make this work a practical investment guide rather than a scholarly text. For those who do want to study these issues further, we offer the following set of references. They are organized by chapter. Where certain references are cited throughout the book, they are listed only in the first chapter in which they were used.

PART I: THE RICHES TO BE REAPED

Chapter One:
Investment Opportunities Flourish Outside the Developed World

"China's New Model Army," *The Economist,* June 11, 1994.

Curran, John, "China's Investment Boom," *Fortune,* March 7, 1994.

Economist Intelligence Unit (EIU), *Country Report, Chile,* 1996.

International Finance Corporation, *Emerging Stock Market Fact Book,* 1994.

McDonough, William J., "Asia and the World Economy—A Central Banker's Perspective," Distinguished Lecture, The Inaugural Hong Kong Monetary Authority, Dec. 3, 1996.

McNamee, Mark, "The In-Your-Face Economist at the World Bank," *Business Week,* May 11, 1992.

Naisbitt, John, *Megatrends Asia* (New York: Simon & Schuster, 1996).

Nixon, Richard, *Beyond Peace* (New York: Random House, 1994).

Overholt, William, *The Rise of China* (New York: Norton, 1993).

Rohwer, Jim, *Rising Asia* (New York: Simon & Schuster, 1996).

"Slim Picking from China's Financial Takeaway," *The Economist,* Feb. 11, 1995.

Song, Byung-Nak, *The Rise of the Korean Economy* (New York: Oxford University Press, 1990).

Swiss Bank Corporation Research, *Fortnightly Review,* January 13, 1993.

Thurow, Lester, *The Future of Capitalism* (New York: Morrow, 1996).

Tyler, Patrick, "China Migrants: Economic Engine, Social Burden," *New York Times,* June 29, 1994.

WuDunn, Sheryl, and Nicholas Kristof, *China Wakes* (New York: Times Books, 1995).

CHAPTER TWO:
The Price Is Right on the Other Side

Holmes, Kim, Bryan Johnson, and Melanie Kirkpatrick, "Index of Economic Freedom," The Heritage Foundation and *The Wall Street Journal,* 1997.

Krugman, Paul, "The Myth of Asia's Miracle," in *Pop Internationalism* (Cambridge, Mass.: MIT Press, 1996).

Lynch, Peter, *One Up on Wall Street* (New York: Simon & Schuster, 1988).

Smith Barney & Company, *Global Asset Allocator,* 1996.

Vogel, Ezra, *The Four Little Dragons* (Cambridge, Mass.: Harvard University Press, 1991).

Weidenbaum, Murray, and Samuel Hughes, *The Bamboo Network* (New York: Free Press, 1996).

World Bank, "Financial Flows and Developing Countries," 1996.

PART II: THE DANGERS TO BE AVOIDED

CHAPTER THREE:
Political Instability Can Sour Many an Investment Opportunity

Brown, Archie, Michael Kaser, and Gerald Smith, *The Cambridge Encyclopedia of Russia* (London: Cambridge University Press, 1994).

Brown, Stephen, William Goetzmann, and Stephen Ross, "Survival," *Journal of Finance,* 50 (1995), pp. 853–874.

Burns, John F., "Fowl Fight over Flies Sends India into a Stew," *New York Times,* Nov. 25, 1995.

Council of the Corporation of Foreign Bondholders, *Annual Report,* 1971.

Davies, Emil, *Investments Abroad* (New York: A.W. Shaw Company, 1927).

Dukes, Paul, *A History of Russia* (Durham: Duke University Press, 1990).

Encarta, "Russian Revolution," Microsoft, 1994.

———, "Colonies and Colonialism," Microsoft, 1994.

Gardner, J., "Foreign Investment and the War," *Financial Review of Reviews* (London), December 1915.

Gatrell, Peter, *Government, Industry, and Rearmament in Russia 1900–1914* (New York: Cambridge University Press, 1994).

Goetzmann, William, and Philippe Jorion, "A Century of Global Stock Markets," Working Paper, Yale University.

———, "Re-emerging Markets," Working Paper, Yale University.

Ibbotson, Roger, and Gary Brinson, *Global Investing* (New York: McGraw-Hill, 1993).

Kimber, Albert, *Foreign Government Securities* (New York: A. W. Kimber & Company, 1919).

Lyashchenko, Peter, *History of the National Economy of Russia* (New York: Octagon Books, 1970).

Park, Keith, and Antoine Van Agtmael, *The World's Emerging Stock Markets* (Chicago: Probus Publishing Company, 1993).

Poole, Claire, "The Next Chile," *Forbes,* Aug. 31, 1992.

Smith, Roy, *The Global Bankers* (New York: Truman Talley Books, 1989).

———, and Ingo Walter, "Rethinking Emerging Markets," *The Washington Quarterly,* Winter 1996.

Solnik, Bruno, *International Investments* (New York: Addison-Wesley, 1996).

Statistical Abstract of the United States, 1915.

Chapter Four:
Lawlessness Makes Emerging Markets a Dangerous Jungle

Bohlen, Celestine, "A New Russia: Now Thrive the Swindlers," *New York Times,* Mar. 17, 1994.

Bray, Nicholas, and Carlta Vitzthum, "Money Games," *Wall Street Journal,* Feb. 2, 1994.

Dillon, Sam, "Zedillo Lectures the Mexicans: Obey the Law," *New York Times,* Oct. 1, 1996.

"Emerging Market Indicators," *The Economist,* Mar. 1996.

"India Arrests a Broker as Stock Scandal Widens," *Wall Street Journal,* June 6, 1992.

Dubey, Suman, "Indian Scandal Mires Standard Chartered," *Wall Street Journal,* Aug. 11, 1992.

———, "India Raises Its Estimate of Losses in Stock Scandal," *Asian Wall Street Journal,* July 13, 1992.

———, "Investigators Say Scandal in India Is Broader Than First Reported," *Asian Wall Street Journal,* June 1, 1992.

———, "Notorious Indian Broker Rose with Boom in Market and Is Now Blamed for Its Fall," *Asian Wall Street Journal,* May 25, 1992.

Erlanger, Steve, "Risks of Russia's Young Markets," *New York Times,* August 5, 1994.

Galuszka, Peter, "Look Who's Making a Revolution: Shareholders," *Business Week,* Feb. 20, 1995.

Glain, Steve, "Korea's Rush to Build Invites Tragedy; Store Collapse Is Latest Example of Shoddy Construction," *Wall Street Journal,* July 6, 1995.

Karas, Veronika, "The Collapse of the MMM," Term Paper, New York University, 1995.

Kim, Harold, and J. P. Mei, "What Makes the Stock Market Jump?," Working Paper, New York University, 1996.

Klebnikov, Paul, "Russia—the Ultimate Emerging Market," *Forbes,* Feb. 14, 1994.

McDonald, Hamish, "A Load of Bull: India's Share Market Set for a Steep Fall," *Far Eastern Economic Review,* Apr. 9, 1992.

Mobius, Mark, *Mobius on Emerging Markets* (London: Financial Times, 1996).

Moshavi, Sharon, "Get the Foreign Devils," *Business Week,* Oct. 23, 1995.

Nakarami, Laxmi, "Paralysis in South Korea," *Business Week,* June 8, 1992.

Perlez, Jane, "Eastern Europe, Post Communism: Five Years Later—A Special Report," *New York Times,* Oct. 7, 1994.

"Ponzi, by Any Other Name," *The Economist,* Sept. 18, 1993.

Smith, Craig, "Bets Are On in China, Though Wagering Is Forbidden by Beijing," *Wall Street Journal,* Feb. 20, 1996.

Specter, Michael, "A Russian Pyramid Collapses: Burying Belief in Capitalism," *New York Times,* July 28, 1994.

Stanley, Alessandra, "Day 5 in a Sinking Stock Pyramid: Blame Moscow," *New York Times,* Aug. 2, 1994.

Wagstyll, Stefan, "Bombay Securities Scandal: Harshad Mehta, Determined to Clear His Name," *Financial Times,* Oct. 2, 1992.

CHAPTER FIVE:

Volatility Guarantees a Bumpy Investment Ride

"Before the Fall," *The Economist,* Oct. 16, 1993.

Bekaert, Geert, and Campbell Harvey, "Emerging Equity Market Volatility," Working Paper, Stanford University, 1996.

Chen, Kathy, "Rioting Brings Halt to Trading in Chinese City," *Wall Street Journal,* August 1992.

Jackson, Ted, "Tourist Attraction," *Financial World,* July 8, 1996.

Malkiel, Burton, *A Random Walk Down Wall Street,* 6th ed. (New York: Norton, 1996).

McGregor, James, "China's Officials Think They Have Tools to Take Risk Out of Stocks," *Wall Street Journal,* May 20, 1992.

Quinn, Andrew, "Taiwan Bourse Hits Record Despite Gloomy Fortune Tellers," Reuters, Sept. 7, 1989.

Schlesinger, David, "Taiwan's Money Fever Makes It Republic of Casino," Reuters, Sept. 11, 1989.

"Taiwan: The Big Hands on the Taipei Stock Market Are Turning Their Attention to Other Asian Markets," *Asia Money,* Oct. 25, 1990.

Wickenden, Peter, "Taipei Stock Market Gamblers Come to Grief," *Financial Times,* May 3, 1990.

CHAPTER SIX:

How Diversification Can Reduce Risk

Bailey, Warren, and Rene Stulz, "Benefits of International Diversification: The Case of Pacific Basin Stock Markets," *Journal of Portfolio Management,* Summer 1990.

Divecha, Arjun, Jaime Drach, and Dan Stefek, "Emerging Markets, A Quantitative Perspective," *Journal of Portfolio Management,* Fall 1992.

Harvey, Campbell, "Predictable Risk and Returns in Emerging Markets," *Review of Financial Studies,* 1995, 8, pp. 773–816.

Jorion, Philippe, "International Portfolio Diversification with Estimation Risk," *Journal of Business,* July 1985, pp. 259–278.

Michaud, Richard, Gary Bergstrom, Ronald Frashure, and Brian Wolahan, "Twenty Years of International Equity Investing," *Journal of Portfolio Management,* Fall 1996.

Senchack, Andrew, and William Beedles, "Is Indirect International Diversification Desirable?," *Journal of Portfolio Management,* Winter 1990.

Speidell, Lawrence, and Ross Sappenfield, "Global Diversification in a Shrinking World," *Journal of Portfolio Management,* Fall 1992.

PART III: HOW TO INVEST IN EMERGING MARKETS

CHAPTER SEVEN:

The Professionally Managed Approach

Bailey, Warren, and Joseph Lim, "Evaluating the Diversification Benefits of the New Country Funds," *Journal of Portfolio Management,* Spring 1992.

Bekaert, Geert, and Michael Urias, "Diversification, Integration, and Emerging Market Closed-End Funds," *Journal of Finance,* July 1995, pp. 835–871.

CHAPTER EIGHT:
The Indexed, or Computer-Managed, Approach

Claessens, Stijn, Susmita Dasgupta, and Jack Glen, "Return Behavior in Emerging Stock Markets," *World Bank Review,* 1995, pp. 131–151.

Malkiel, Burton, "Indexing: Implications for Financial Analysis," *Journal of Financial Statement Analysis,* Summer 1996.

Schoenfeld, Steven, "Fund Manager May Get Benched," *Far Eastern Economic Review,* Sept. 12, 1996.

CHAPTER NINE:
The Self-Directed Approach: Actively Managing Your Emerging-Market Portfolio

Bakaert, Geert, Claude Erb, Campbell Harvey, and Tadas Viskanta, "The Behavior of Emerging Market Returns," *NYU Emerging Market Conference Volume,* 1997.

Erb, Claude, Campbell Harvey, and Tadas Viskanta, "Expected Return and Volatility in 135 Countries," Journal of Portfolio Management, 1996.

——, "Political Risk, Economic Risk, and Financial Risk," Working Paper, Duke University, 1996.

Gardner, Grant, and Thierry Wuilloud, "Currency Risk in International Portfolios: How Satisfying Is Optimal Hedging?" *Journal of Portfolio Management,* Spring 1995.

Harvey, Campbell, "Portfolio Enhancement Using Emerging Markets and Conditioning Information," *Portfolio Investment in Developing Countries,* 1992.

Hauser, Shmuel, Matityahu Marcus, and Uzi Yaari, "Investing in Emerging Stock Markets: Is It Worthwhile Hedging Foreign Exchange Risk?" *Journal of Portfolio Management,* Spring 1994.

Smith, Barney, "Emerging Market Equity Allocator," June 1996.

CHAPTER TEN:
Bargains in Bonds, Real Estate, and Natural Resources

Bernstein, Robert, and John Penicook, "Emerging Market Debt: Practical Portfolio Considerations," *NYU Emerging Market Conference Volume,* 1997.

"The Erection Index," *The Economist,* May 11, 1996.

Liu, Crocker, and J. P. Mei, "Evidence on the Integration of International Markets and Benefits of Diversification," *Real Estate Economics,* 1997.

Prudential Real Estate Investors, "The China Report," 1994.

Quan, Daniel, and Sheridan Titman, "Commercial Real Estate Prices and Stock Market Returns: An International Analysis," Working Paper, University of Texas, 1996.

CHAPTER ELEVEN:
Investment Strategies and Specific Recommendations

Jagannathan, Ravi, and Narayana Kocherlakota, "Why Should Older People Invest Less in Stocks Than Younger People?," *Federal Reserve Bank of Minneapolis Review,* Summer 1996.

Acknowledgments

IN PREPARING THIS manuscript we have been very fortunate to have the assistance of many individuals who contributed to our research and who were helpful in countless other ways. We could not have completed *Global Bargain Hunting* without their invaluable contributions.

We have benefited greatly from the helpful comments and suggestions of colleagues from the academic and investment communities. Several individuals read the entire manuscript and made extremely useful suggestions. These included James Garland, Garnett Keith, William Bethke, Leila Heckman, James Litvack, John Ammer, Warren Bailey, David Woolford, Paul Appleby, Lewis R. Hood, Sari Carp, and especially John Campbell. Their comments went far beyond the usual call of duty and have greatly enriched the content of this book. We also are grateful to Barton Biggs, Gregory Chow, Chrysa DaCosta, Wang Daohan, Madhav Dhar, Campbell Harvey, Richard Levich, John Levin, Crocker Liu, Mike Miles, John Mullen, Martha Farnsworth Riche, Whitney Rogers, Roy Smith, Shang Song, Ingo Walter, Byron Wien, Richard Williams, Lin Zhou, and William Y. M. Zhou for very helpful discussions and assistance.

We are particularly indebted to Walter Lenhard, William Norris, and George Sauter of The Vanguard Group, Rodney Alldredge of Daniels & Alldredge, and Lawrence Larkin of Barings for assistance in helping us obtain data used in many of the analyses we undertook.

Many students helped us in performing essential research. These included Elizabeth Brill, Sari Carp, Nancy Ficca, Brian Jo,

Kristen Johnson, Veronika Karas, Lara Larson, Joshua Ross, Melody Tsai, and Jimmy Wu.

Douglas Daniels, Esq., provided important legal advice, and our editor at Simon & Schuster, Frederic Hills, made numerous suggestions that improved our manuscript significantly. Patricia Taylor, a professional writer and editor, read through two complete drafts of the manuscript and made many suggestions of both style and substance. Ms. Taylor had an especially important influence on the book's organization. Nancy Weiss Malkiel also read through two drafts and made critically important contributions to the clarity and style of the exposition, as well as providing countless creative ideas. Lynn Anderson and Leslie Ellen provided enormously effective and understanding copy editing. No writers could have been blessed with more intelligent, capable, and unrelenting editors.

Lugene Whitley flawlessly typed several drafts of each chapter and kept track of the countless exhibits, graphs, tables, cartoons, and pictures that are included herein. Phyllis Durepos also contributed importantly by producing some of the earliest drafts from illegible handwriting. Laurel Cantor and Isabella Arregui contributed the picture montage of defaulted securities displayed in Chapter Three. Hilary Black was helpful in many ways.

J. P. Mei especially wishes to acknowledge the love and education in traditional values imparted by his grandparents, Mei Guangyun and Xu Shizhen, as well as the support of Gregory Chow, who brought him from China to the United States. We both want to thank our wives, Nancy and Wei, who provided incomparable love and support, and our children, Jonathan and Grayce.

INDEX

About the Authors

BURTON G. MALKIEL holds the Chemical Bank Chairman's Professorship in the Economics Department of Princeton University. He is the author of seven books, including the best-selling *A Random Walk Down Wall Street*. From 1975 to 1977, he served as a member of President Ford's Council of Economic Advisers, and from 1981 through 1987 was Dean of the Yale School of Management. Malkiel sits on seven corporate boards of directors, including Prudential Insurance Company, The Vanguard Group of Investment Companies, Amdahl, and SNET.

J. P. MEI was born in Shanghai, China. In his youth, he was an enthusiastic "Little Red Guard" during the Cultural Revolution, but he has grown up to become a diehard preacher of free markets. Currently, he is an associate professor of finance at the Stern School of Business at New York University. He specializes in asset pricing and has particular expertise in Asian stock and real estate markets. He has written two books and a large number of articles in professional journals